Plant Your Feet Firmly in Mid-Air

"This is a book to read, mark, study, and read again. It offers the clear, practical, and realistic guidance needed by today's leaders." –Horst Schulze, CEO, Ritz-Carlton Hotel Company

"This book gives clear, common sense advice on managing technology, and overcoming others' resistance to change. I highly recommend it to anyone concerned about how to manage people." –Dan Burrus, Author, *Technotrends*.

"Pragmatic, readable, step-by-step guides to helping both oneself and others move through a chaotic and unpredictable time. Dr. Janet Lapp offers new ways of thinking and a fresh approach to change." –Dave Hubers, CEO, American Express Financial Services

Plant Your Feet Firmly In Mid-Air

Guidance Through Turbulent Change

Janet E. Lapp, PhD

Demeter Business Books

Library of Congress Publisher's Cataloging-In-Publication Data
Lapp, Janet E.

Plant your feet firmly in mid-air: Guidance through turbulence change /
Janet E. Lapp
        p.cm.
     Includes bibliographic references and index.
     ISBN 1-885365-00-4
      1. Organizational change–Management. 2. Personnel
management. 3. Organizational effectiveness. I.Title   II. Title.

58.8 L36 1996
658.4   CIP 95-71616

This book is available at a special discount when ordered in bulk quanti-
ties. For information, contact Demeter Press, Post Office Box 2583, Del
Mar, California 92014-5583.

Printing number
10 9 8 7 6 5 4 3 2 1
First printing, September 1996

Foreword

Plant your Feet Firmly in Mid-Air:
Guidance Through Turbulent Change
by Jeff Davidson

Plant Your Feet Firmly in Mid-Air addresses how to develop the skills needed in the modern organization, to build and re-build trust, to develop an effective leadership style for the new era, to overcome resistance to change, and to employ new ways of thinking. This is not a book about management theory; rather, it is a book that offers real solutions to the very real problems that managers, executives, and entrepreneurs, face on a daily basis.

The author identifies and explains personal mastery skills to guide you through current turbulent changes toward productive outcomes. The principles and practices outlined in this book can make you a better manager of behavioral change than you are today.

Dr. Janet Lapp is a gifted observer of structures, dynamics and people. With clarity, wit, style and insight, she shows employees and managers how to thrive in the throes of change. I highly recommend this book to anyone seeking clear and helpful information about guiding today's organizations.

To my grandchildren
Christopher and Hayley, with love.

Contents

Introduction

The premise of this book is that even though many organizations appear to have joined the 'new wave,' or the new way of doing business, their people and management systems are stuck in the first wave, that is, in the old way of doing business and of managing people. The dissonance created by these two competing systems has created unprecedented and uncomfortable turbulence in today's corporation. It is as if two storm fronts are clashing, and although we know the air will be turbulent, it is nonetheless confusing, and occasionally frightening. This book was designed to guide through this current dissonance created by two competing systems toward the calmer weather of consonance and stability.

Unfortunately, many of the familiar guideposts are missing as we travel. Imagine you are seated comfortably in an airline seat, waiting at the gate. You watch the luggage and meals being loaded, hear the familiar announcements, and feel the push back, taxi and take-off. You enjoy the topography of the land as it zooms out of view. But then, suddenly, everything becomes clouded. You lose all sense of position. Nothing is anchored. There are no indicators to judge distance. You have simply to trust that the pilot is taking you to your destination.

If you are the pilot, however, a different picture emerges. There are reliable guides through the clouds. Even when the sky is occluded, pilots believe their instruments can lead them faithfully to their destination. Similarly, even though transformational change can be described as leaving the known and venturing into the unknown, there are instruments to guide us, as well. Much of the skill upon which I have relied as an instrument pilot can be transferred to guiding change in times of confusion and ambiguity, and this is the source and focus of much of my writing.

This book developed for two primary reasons: first, I became dissatisfied with materials presently available to help people during the chaotic changes in today's companies. Many materials offer theories which, although intriguing and perhaps heuristically useful, nonetheless do little to guide today's manager. In *Plant Your Feet Firmly in Mid-Air*, I have tried to outline clear steps toward change, and offer suggestions that today's managers and staff persons can follow. The second reason this book developed, was to try to help alleviate the real pain and confusion I observe throughout North America when I travel and work with various corporations and associations. At the same time, I am awed by the herculean efforts of courageous people in today's companies who are valiantly trying to cope with uncertainty, confusion and overwork. There are masses of employees at all levels who exhibit a committed caring about their work and their fellow workers. These people don't need theories! They need real answers, strategies, ways of thinking and acting based on common-sense to help them steer through turbulence. I believe that this book addresses those people and their needs, while simultaneously offering their leaders the tools to better guide them.

Richard Pascale, in *Managing on the Edge* (1993), argues that the complex messages eluding us these days is common-sense, and that there are not, and never have been, short-cuts to 'good management.' Additionally, to really understand how highly rated companies work, we also need to study why others can fail. Chapter One examines some of the possible causes for failure.

Some challenges to current common-sense seem to be that the the most popular business gurus reflect North America's obsession with the *new*. Similar to some psychotherapies, in which the very newness of a therapeutic technique provides the cure, there is the admonition in business circles to 'hurry up and use the new technique while it still works.' The generated hope can gather enough momentum and power to act as a placebo. Tom Peters captured this 'new' spirit when he coined the axiom, 'Get Innovative or Get Dead.' But unfortunately, subjecting any organization to repeated epidemics of 'hit or miss,' trial-and-error roller coasters, replete with fancy jargon, demoralizes employees, confuses customers and eventually, obscures the very purpose of the business.

Ray Rasmussen, from the University of Alberta, has stated that in hawking trendy ideas such as 'excellence,' 'seven habits' and 'learning organizations,' business gurus all too often ignore the sweat and tears–the human factors–it takes to manage a company well. For example, Tom Peters and Robert Waterman Jr.'s *In Search of Excellence* (Peters & Waterman, 1982), identified the so-called immutable secrets of excellence in 43 companies. Yet, five years later, most of the anointed companies were no longer considered excellent and some, such as Atari Corp., Digital Equipment Corp., Revlon Inc., Avon Products Inc., Wang Laboratories Inc. and IBM Corp., have even experienced some quite un-excellent adventures.

According to Drucker (1980), organizations operate on a set of sacred, unwritten, powerful and pervasive assumptions. Unless this set of corporate beliefs shift along with other changes, quick-fixes in the form of Total Quality Management, Total Customer Service and similar programs, may do more harm than good. To create new organizations with staying power, that can create jobs for the future, and growth for our economies, the corporate mind-set must change. Chapter Seven offers several suggestions on how to overcome blocked corporate culture and vision.

Michael Hammer and Jim Champy in *Re-engineering the Corporation: A Manifesto for Business Revolution* admit that 70% of re-engineering efforts fail to achieve any desired results (Hammer & Champy, 1994). One reason they propose for this is that everyone involved in a process looks inward toward their department and upward toward their boss, but no one looks outward toward the customer. Chapters Four to Six in this book provides guidance toward recognizing and serving the 'New Customer' with an info-business, more speed, and by building a better path.

In Chapter Eight we see that control over our own behavior and some perceived control over our environment, is central to change taking hold and becoming fundamental. The more control we have or perceive, the more willing we are to risk further change.

The leaders who make the biggest difference in today's organizations are those who, regardless of job or level, determine how to inspire people through the dynamics of change itself. Chapter Ten gives guidance on how to develop the leadership behaviors that today's organization needs.

Unless genuine culture change accompanies process redesign, improvements will be typically ineffectual and short-lived. Re-engineering does not focus on the leadership skills needed for change. The leaders' behavior is fundamental to creating and sustaining a truly successful alteration in course and direction. Chapters Eleven and Twelve will help you to guide yourself and others through change.

If you wish to manage individuals during change, it is important to learn how to overcome resistance to change and increase the control over their work places. Chapters Fourteen and Fifteen address resistance to change, and gives suggestions on how to help others climb on board the change effort.

However, one caveat: by nature, change is chaotic. One can't ever completely manage it, control it, or master it. One can only recognize that it is unpredictable and shapeless in its essence, and that no book, method, seminar, or course of study will ever make it completely comfortable and clear. But what we *can* do is to understand that it is *not* understandable, and learn to adjust to the unfamiliarity and ambiguity of it.

This book can help anyone in an organization faced with learning new and different ways of effecting, and coping with, change, whether a front-line employee who has to learn different practices of operation, communication, or service, someone in finance, sales, marketing, research, or engineering now needing new skills, or a supervisor or manager in a small to mid-size company charged with leading change.

Most importantly, this is not a book about what's wrong. It is a book about what is right, hopeful, and workable. The principles identified and explained herein can make you a much better guide of behavioral change than you already are. I hope this book guides you on your journey to an exciting future.

San Diego, California
June, 1996

 P.S. These feet have been planted throughout the text, to signify important exercises that will serve as your guideposts through change. Whenever you encounter the feet, do the exercise, or answer the questions posed. Taking the time for the exercises will increase the impact of your experience with this book. Thanks, and enjoy your journey. J.L.

Plant Your Feet Firmly in Mid-Air

Chapter One
Why Change?

*In my opinion, there are two kinds of businesses
in the United States: those that are heading
for the cliff and know it, and those that are heading
the same way but don't know it.*
Jack Welch

The pace of change is accelerating daily. Change has changed. We cannot envision the future. As McCluhan (1966) has said "We don't know what's happening to us, and that's what is happening to us."

The Time to Change
Perhaps your revenue growth is flat, perhaps new competitors have shown up with a new technology. Both these represent the 'second curve' (Morrison, 1996), or the second wave of business reflecting the 'new paradigm.' This new wave is fueled by new technologies, new markets and new consumers–things cannot revert to the way they were.

The time to change is before the Second Curve (Morrison, 1996), or Inflection Point (Grove, 1996), that is, before the point where change becomes mandatory because revenue is sliding. If your company is too big or too successful to fail, you may need to change the most radically. For example, the

IBM of 1985 was on top of their market, but in 1987 lost 25% of market share to Compaq, who are now leading in worldwide sales. IBM's main failing? Isolationism, or the refusal to believe that others could do it better. Although they are now beginning to rally, they lost millions because they would not give up what initially made them great. The Canadian National and Canadian Pacific Railways made attempts to switch to the vision of 'transportation' instead of 'railroad.' They diversified, looked to new revenue streams, but they never made the emotional switch; they loved trains too much, and wouldn't give up what made them great. Are *you* working for a K-Mart of 1980, a Sears of 1960, an IBM of 1970, or an Apple Computer of 1985?

The greatest mistake is to do more of what one
has always done because it's always worked.

IBM's challenges began after a string of successes, which is a dangerous position for any company. They lost touch with reality; their central planning and lack of accountability given to the field contributed to their lack of awareness. Employees, with 80% of their cost assigned, didn't assume responsibility for profits or losses.

Similarly, the cattle industry enjoyed ten years of living, 'high on the hog,' ignoring growing competition from other meats, vegetarianism, other proteins, and ethnic foods. They could have retained dominance and survived economically as long as conditions had remained unchanged; however, with current global competition, low cattle prices and high grain prices, they now must make drastic changes toward partnering, lowering costs, weeding out inefficiencies, and standardizing product to remain competitive.

Never rest. Success is a signal to put in even more effort.

Have You Reached the Crossover or Inflection Point?

Similar to other living things, companies have a life cycle with crossover points during which there are dramatic shifts. The beginning of the life cycle curve typically involves learning and investment, and the end is characterized by diminishing returns. The challenge is to understand when it is time to make changes and to move to a different level, or form. There are key times when these changes must be made. When they are missed, the organism suffers and often, cannot survive.

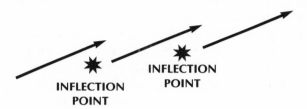

INFLECTION
POINT

INFLECTION
POINT

Intel CEO Andrew Grove (Doubleday, 1996) explains that there is a critical time for every company to jump to the next s-curve. It has to do with the strategic inflection point—the point in the middle of a sideways S-shaped curve where the curve changes from one side to the other. If you chart the life of any industry, company or career, you'll see these points of great change; points of biggest upset and turmoil. Intel, for instance, hit a strategic inflection point in the 1980's, when the Japanese began crushing Intel in the company's original business of making DRAM memory chips. Intel abandoned DRAMs and focused on more sophisticated microprocessors. The decision paved the way for Intel's current success. Grove's book focuses on how to recognize such points and make the best of them.

Similarly, there is at least one point in the evolution of any system when conditions are such that a drastic change to a new level is needed. There was a time when Detroit noticed that America was buying Japanese cars, IBM noticed that the industry was moving away from large mainframes, Sears saw its first Wal Mart, Big Steel saw its product turned into a commodity, and the electric utilities noticed their first Independent Power Producer. The time for decisions was at the juncture, but most waited until the S-curve peaked and are now scrambling to catch up.

> *Absence of alternatives clears the mind tremendously.*
> Henry Kissinger

One useful analogy for this phenomenon is 'epigenesis'*, a biological phenomenon that has been useful in understanding the patterned flow in all life cycles. It is equally applicable to individuals as organizations. Psychologist Erik Erikson used this notion to spell out the various phases of a person's life cycle. Each of the tasks of development need to be met before an individual can move successfully to the next stage. The oft quoted Ecclesiastes 3:2 "a time to plant and a time to pluck what is planted," has addressed a similar theme. Each season of life has it's appropriate task. Whether biology, psychology, farming, religion, or business, ones does not sow in autumn and reap in spring.

 If you are in a mature industry such as in one of the utilities or automobile industry, ask yourself:
Where is our company in its life cycle?
What are we doing to seed the next generation of business?

> *We were the ones who made the rules, and we had*
> *rules about everything. Our culture had no instinct for*
> *competition. People believed that if you got a job here,*
> *it was a lifetime opportunity. We had an entitlement*
> *philosophy, believing that we were a monopoly*
> *because it was right to be a monopoly.*
> A Senior VP in the Bell system

 These feet are planted throughout the text, to signify exercises to do or questions to ask yourself. They are important guideposts through change.

---

*Epigenesis holds that embryos are created entirely new and develop in a determined way. The lenses of the eyes, for example, are supposed to appear in the seventh week of gestation, but if they don't, they are not going to pop up in the seventeenth week. The message is that if things don't develop at their appropriate time, they are not going to develop at a later one.

Another reason for learning where you are in your life cycle is to avoid the build-up of organizational 'plaque,' or company residue. Only when old systems, thoughts, rules, and beliefs are discarded, can businesses stay ahead of their organizations. If they don't, the organization can overtake the business and bureaucracy grows.

W. Edwards Deming (1986) has said,
"The kind of management being practiced in American corporations now, and being taught at American business schools, is the biggest producer of waste, causing huge losses whose magnitude cannot be evaluated or measured. Most people in management are not aware that they are imprisoned by current practices of management ... that these management practices are the cause of American corporate decline. (These practices) prevent companies from functioning efficiently as a system."

> *They can have any color Model T*
> *they want as long as it's black.*
> Henry Ford

While it may not at first be apparent or believable, business problems are less a matter of fixing external factors than doing what is needed internally. One of the reasons why management is unable to change is the inability to let go of old practices.

> *Businesses fail not because they don't know*
> *what to do. They fail because they*
> *don't know what to give up.*
> Peter Drucker

For nostalgic reasons, I often visit Canadian Tire stores whenever I visit my family in Canada, because they are not much different in 1996 than they were in 1950. During a recent visit to an Ontario store, clerks were stocking shelves during store hours, leaving unopened and undisplayed merchandise boxes in the aisles, and customer assistance was not to be had. It's uncertain what is holding back Canadian Tire from entering the future. If Canadian Tire succumbs to growing competition, it may not just be lack of focus, it could be that no-one has updated the old belief that customer service is not primary.

The struggle to hold on is just as powerful for nations and for businesses, as it is for people. It is a human tendency to want to hang on to what has worked in the past, but it is a skill of today to learn to let go. Inability to let go may be the single most compelling reason for failure, both personally and professionally.

On a cash register in Des Moines, Iowa:
Don't look back, we ain't going there.

But, as the Bob Dylan song lyrics state: "You don't have to be a weatherman to know which way the wind blows," general trends have surfaced that are not difficult to track. Browse through the shifts on the following page to develop a sense of current structural changes in today's organizations.

When Business Misses the Change Point
When things go wrong, executives, like other people, typically blame external factors—unions, attitudes, costs, government interference. This belies a belief that the magic solution will be found from an outside source. But while current external challenges don't make it easy to do business, they have not been found to be the cause of decline. Robert Hayes's 1994 analysis of American industries, showed that an organization's failure to compete has little to do with economic, governmental, cultural, or labor issues. It is primarily a failure of management.

According to Martin (1993), the key to the process is self-examination. Even educated professionals prevent change by engaging in organizational defensive routines to preserve sta-

OLD WAVE	NEW WAVE
Incremental change	Fundamental change
Bottom line of last quarter	Percent of global market share
Job titles	Job skills
Job security	Job adaptability
Doing it right the first time	Experimentation/failure
Long-term planning	Short cycle times
Price, paying for products	Speed, paying for time
Valuing material wealth	Valuing free time
More information	Focused information
Design for assembly	Design for disassembly
Thinking global	Being global
Vertical, rigid hierarchies	Horizontal, flexible networks
Excess	Minimalism
Consensus-building	Critical-mass leadership
Good customer service	Exceptional service
Focus on input	Focus on output
Vertical integration	Intelligence departments
Yearly forecasts	Month-by-month projections
Doing things the same way	Open conflict and dissension
Long meetings	Quick brainstorm meetings
TQM and Excellence training	Communication, problem solving, conflict
Pessimism	Optimism
Learning content	Learning *how to learn*
Internal focus on the boss	Focus on the customer
What to do	*How* to do
Announcing changes	Describing change to employees before designing it
Jumping on the latest fad	Researching what will work
Insisting everyone climb on board before moving	Working first with those who accept change the most easily, then with next level, and letting the tide of change drag along resistors.

tus and security. One recent study found that 95% of failing companies blamed poor economic conditions, and only 13% said poor management had anything to do with present problems. Organizations defend against change because they are made up of individuals who are working at what 'always has worked.' Companies, like individuals, think that to change means that they have been wrong all these years. Not so.

This faulty attribution is similar to when one faces a mirror, and seeing a blemish, wipes the mirror in an effort to remove the blemish. Sooner or later, one discovers that the blemish is not on the mirror. The remedy is to remove the blemish from your own skin, not to spend time removing the reflection in the mirror.

Management's failure to do internal work
is usually found to be the primary
causative factor leading to defeat.

These are the top 13 reasons why a business gets into trouble. Notice that the top seven reasons result from simple lack of attention and/or a failure to 'let go,' the next three (Nos. 8-10) from lack of training, and only the last three have anything to do with economics.

1.   Shifts or changes in marketplace
2.   Inadequate control systems
3.   Changes in technology
4.   Precipitous change in distribution system
5.   Abrupt location disadvantages
6.   Over-dependence on single customer
7.   Growth of business beyond skills of management
•••••••••••••••••••••••••••••••••••
8.   Management short of courage
9.   Internal conflicts
10.   A group exerts selfish influence
•••••••••••••••••••••••••••••••••••
11.   Limited financial resources

12.   Growth beyond working capital
13.   An increase in cost of debt

Low Medicare and Medicaid payments didn't close over 100 hospitals last year, a link espoused by hospital industry executives, and swallowed by the media. The blame, in many cases, rested with hospital executives who waited too long to respond to changes in their market. Poor management has been responsible for at least half of the recent hospital closings. Despite changes in their markets, many troubled hospitals waited too long to adapt to those changes.

What Went Wrong?
One criticism of abandoned re-engineering efforts is that there is typically no analysis of why the effort failed. A 1995 AMA study of more than 150 new products concluded that 'the knowledge gained from failures [is] often instrumental in achieving subsequent successes.... In the simplest terms, failure is the ultimate teacher.' Most of us learn through our errors rather than our successes. Thus, it could be heuristically useful to analyze the most serious system errors that most commonly lead to derailment.When these have been ignored, the consequences have been, at times, disastrous. At the very least, painful consequences could have been averted had these errors been tracked.

For example, IBM became a world-wide 380,000-member employment club, while its mainframe business went flat. Coca-Cola Co. wasn't paying attention to its German-made miniature soda fountain BreakMates. Someone forgot that Coca-Cola's business was large volume, the deutsche mark rose, but Coke pushed doggedly on.The Limited and Victoria's Secret deteriorated while Leslie Wexner was distracted by outside pursuits. While he engaged in outside political interests and limited-market consumer electronics, Apple Computer Inc. John Sculley's one-foot-in-one-foot-out management style left Apple Computer in the dust. Once you lose focus, it's hard to regain it.

A pilot doesn't notice that she is 45 degrees of course because she has fixated on a malfunctioning attitude indicator. A non-instrument-rated pilot ignores increasingly menacing weather, pushes on into the clouds, then spirals out of control.

Successful companies, like successful pilots, examine their failures. Xerox examined three troubled products in an effort to understand why the company's new business initiatives failed so often. British Petroleum established a post-project appraisal unit to review major investment projects, write up case studies, and derive lessons for planners that were then incorporated into revisions of the company's planning guidelines. These companies know that a productive failure is one that leads to insight, understanding, and an addition to the wisdom of the organization. An unproductive success happens when something goes well, but nobody knows how or why.

A framework I use to examine system errors is one that I learned while becoming instrument-rated as a pilot. After observation of companies of all sizes over several years, I have found that there are common system errors to both failure as a pilot and failure in business. When these errors have been recognized and acted upon, the system has righted itself.

Let's return to the instrument flight described in the introduction. We are flying in the clouds. Nothing is familiar. There are no familiar indicators to judge distance and position. If we are the pilots of our aircraft, however, although the world outside the cockpit has become unfamiliar, there are reliable instruments inside that guide us to our destination. If we fail to trust our instruments, we can commit fatal errors. The following are the most common factors involved in fatal accidents in instrument flying. Can you relate them to your current situation in your business or personal life?

1. Fixation

You realize that you have stopped scanning and are staring at just one instrument. Typically, that instrument is malfunctioning and feeding you erroneous information. If it's the Directional Gyro, for example, chances are that you are not only chasing the wrong direction but your altimeter and attitude are seriously off, and you're heading for a spiral.

During stressful periods, animals scan the environment for danger. When stress overloads, the animal may fixate on the most threatening danger signal and ignore the rest. This may be adaptive for small animals, but fatal for business. In business, you find that the one customer who gives you all of your headaches and the least percent of your income, is taking up most of your time. If you're concentrating on one area of your business debt structure, asset deployment, or even on just one client, you may be fixing on a highly troubled low-return area. Pull out and re-focus. You should be scanning constantly, interpreting information, and returning to the area of greatest consequence. One West Coast electric utility put 80% of its trading efforts into a California trading partner who never intended to do significant business with them. Unfortunately, the sheer difficulty of the venture intrigued and obsessed the CEO, and he became fixated. In your personal life, you may have become obsessed with a relationship that is throwing you off-balance. You cannot change the relationship. Get back on course and focus on what you can do, and do have.

Keep scanning all instruments.
Cover up the malfunctioning instrument.

2. Ambiguity

You have information from two independent sources that disagrees and cannot be resolved. Two instruments may contradict each other, but there is typically a third instrument that can verify which of the two is faulty. If you find you are stuck between two sources of information, stop trying to resolve it. Go outside and get further information.

Instead of trying to resolve the discrepancy,
go to a third source to verify it.

3. Complacency

The better you think you're doing, the greater should be your cause for concern. There is never time for rest. That doesn't mean that every time something positive happens to you, you wait for 'the other shoe to drop.' It *does* mean that events occur randomly, and that your grandmother was right: "always expect the best, but prepare for the worst." Real estate developers who became complacent in the 1980's began to understand the concept in the early 1990's when financing dried up.

Fly 'ahead of the plane' and be prepared for the worst
scenario. Be constantly on the lookout for a decent
emergency landing spot.

4. Emotion

If you're ecstatic about a new acquisition, achievement, or relationship–you're emotionally clouded, and may be unsuitable for flight. Give the controls to someone else for a spell. Similarly, if you're depressed, your judgment is clouded. Because emotions are results of thought processes, get the thought processes under control before you fly.

Don't fly when you are emotion focused. Get emotions under
control before you lead others through change.

5. Confusion

You have lost situational awareness and you have a gut feeling that something is not right. This feeling is called a 'pinch.' The worst thing to do is fail to acknowledge your situation and continue to fly blindly. The best thing is to admit your situation and get immediate air traffic control feedback.
Ask for help.

6. Distraction
You are aware that your attention is being drawn to an item that is not really important.

Bring your attention back into focus, immediately.

7. Underload or overload
Similar in concept to #3 (complacency), if the flight is easy or boring, you may not be paying attention to important information. A fellow pilot came too close to a fatal error during his weekly commutes through the Los Angeles basin from San Diego to Monterey, California. With the plane on autopilot, casually reading the newspaper, it wasn't until he was at a 35 degree bank did he notice that his Flight Director was malfunctioning, putting him into a spiral.

Similarly, if you're so busy that you can't think, you are likely to overlook something. One evening in Kansas City, Missouri, because of a blinding snowstorm and ice build-up on the wings, I made an unplanned landing without instrument charts. With an overloaded ATC, the only available assistance were other pilots. Even though they came through at the last minute with instrument approach information, the overload during that time made the approach somewhat of a challenge, and something could have easily been missed.

**For overload or underload, follow your checklist.
Always carry your charts!**

8. Poor communications
Difficulty communicating with ATC or another crew member may indicate that someone does not know what is really occurring. The crew that crashed a jet near Cali, Colombia was misled by an air traffic controller who didn't know where the jet was as it approached the airport. The crash came shortly after the controller told the crew to fly over a radio beacon about 40 miles north of the airport. At the time,

the plane already had passed the beacon. The crew was trying to turn around to go back to the beacon when they impacted the mountain. In this instance, the controller and the crew had different ideas of the airplane's location because of mis-understandings throughout their conversations. Similar to every crash, there was an unusual sequence of events. The controller and pilot didn't understand each other, and the controller was giving clearances that made no sense because he had no radar and could not see the airplane.

Be clear.

9. Failure to meet targets

If you're reaching checkpoint significantly early or late, or if speed or fuel consumption is very different than planned, find out why. In the example above, it was in turning toward the checkpoint that had already passed that impact was made with the mountains.

Keep targets clear, visible to everyone,
and track them frequently.

10. Nobody is flying the aircraft

One of the most reassuring words a student pilot can hear from an instructor is, "I've got it." But many student-instructor fatalities occur when nobody is sure who is flying the plane. With uncertainty, nobody is directing the aircraft, even if it is still flying. Toward the final hours of my instrument training, my instrument instructor and I landed at the busy San Francisco airport. Of course, he assumed that I was tracking and responding to ATC's directions to switch approaches and runways. Because of the traffic, we received several such switches in both instrument approach and run-way use. At one point, I simply let my instructor take over. My error was in not clearly stating that he had the plane. Still under the impression that I was 'in control' my instructor became complacent with heading and approaches. After we landed on the wrong runway, narrowly missed by another aircraft, we were asked to "call the tower." During our mandated conversation we learned that we had seriously erred in the approach, landed on the wrong runway, a Delta Airlines 757 jet had narrowly missed our aircraft and was forced into a go-around.

Clearly indicate who is in control and who is responsible.

In summary, the time to change may be now. Predictable errors are preventable errors. Change may not be as mysterious as you think. The massive global change our world is currently experiencing is similar to biological change, and is thus more predictable and understandable than previously thought. Most biological change happens suddenly. Just prior to the most dramatic and successful biological changes, are periods of upheaval and chaos. The transition period we are currently experiencing, though, however understandable, is nonetheless turbulent and chaotic.

Biological processes are self-organizing systems that balance between order and chaos. Too much order makes change impossible; too much chaos, and there can be no continuity. Changing a living organism such as a company, therefore, is a delicate process requiring wisdom and balance.

Some of the worst mass extinctions happened for no obvious reason. Small evolutionary advantages over another system have been enough to bring down a huge ecosystem. Organizations may disappear from sight for no apparent reason, However, those that are aware of the 'slight edge' phenomenon in biology, tend to survive and continue to be competitive.

An organism cannot let go of anything unless there is a clear pattern for it to follow. Biologically, change occurs when genetic coding permits a new emergent property or form. In my clinical practice, I have found that, to undertake real change, patients have needed permission to let go of the past, a reassurance of their survival during the transition, and a blueprint or model of the new form.

However, the best time to change is not necessarily at the beginning or leading edge of a new trend. The best time to make changes is about one-third of the way through. An airplane wing is constructed so that air flows unevenly over the top and bottom, thus creating a 'suction force' over the wing. Because of the shape of the wing, most of the lift is about one-third of the way back on the wing. The front or leading edge may collect bugs and ice, but doesn't do anything to create lift. The time to take action is at the place of maximum lift potential; about a third of the way behind the start of a new trend.

Begin by anticipating trends and investing 10% of capital and time. Trends are easily anticipated through changes in technology although it isn't any easier to predict future technologies than it is Olympic athletes through baby pictures. You are better positioned to do this if you have been tracking the future and spending at least some of your efforts preparing for it.

Put tomorrow on today's agenda.
Dan Burrus

 Glance back over the notes you've made in the margins of this chapter. Condense them into two action points, or changes you will make.

Actions I will take:

1._____

2._____

Chapter Two
Set Your Course

When I grew up, I always wanted to be somebody.
Now, I wish I'd been more specific.
Lily Tomlin, playing Trudy the Bag Lady in
In 'Search for Intelligent Signs of Life in the Universe.'

As you assess the course of your organization, you will consider these questions: Why should we change? What is there in the environment that creates the urgency? What core changes are needed? What are the biggest issues?

Then you will ask the difficult questions addressed in the upcoming chapters:
a.   Where should we start? What do we focus on? The organization? A department? An individual?
b.   Where are we on the curve? In which direction do we need to go?
c.   What's our basic strategy for moving from one state to another? Do we know enough about the possible techniques?
d.   Who is in charge of the change? We'll need to identify

individuals or a team with clear responsibilities.

e.   What's in it for the individual who changes?

g.   What happens to individuals who don't change?

h.   What will we tell everyone?

Step One
Write A Good Vision or Mission Statement

One way to begin answering these questions is by creating a good vision statement. Despite the caveat expressed in the first chapter concerning the limitations of vision statements--a clear vision, understood by everyone in your organization–is the first and most fundamental step to take before deciding on any change. A lack of a vision statement *that is lived by the organization* is the main reason that organizations go off-track during change. A vision pulls people into the future. There is an old Sufi story of a man who visited a healer, disturbed by a recurring dream. As he explained the dream, he was in a large dark room with an enormous foreboding door with a sign on it. He found himself pushing and straining against the door in an attempt to push it open. The more he pushed, the more frustrated he became. The healer listened patiently, and then inquired as to the writing on the sign. The man replied, "It said *pull*." The writing is on the wall. People move by being pulled. People are not moved by being pushed.

You've read this type of advice many times, but before you dismiss this section–quick–what *is* your mission?

Can you state it right now?
Is it still the right mission?
Is this mission still worth pursuing?

If you are not clear on the answers to these questions, you may not be living by it. You'll be significantly more successful when clearly focused on, and living, a mission every day. Even feisty Lou Gerstner, who said "the last thing IBM needs right now is a vision," is on board with 'IBM Principles.'

If you know it, and you don't do it, you don't know it.

Even though good mission statements are not difficult to create, some organizations spend up to a year on them and yet produce nothing useful. General Motors (GM) spent millions of dollars in staff time and retreat settings to produce the following statement:

The fundamental purpose of (GM) is to provide products and services of such quality that our customers will receive superior value, our employees and business partners will share in our success, and our stockholders will receive a sustained, superior return on their investment.

Would the preceding statement guide employee behavior? Although vision statements may not be tough to create, following through is the creative, challenging part. Ninety-five percent of American managers today say the right thing. Five percent actually do it.

You may not need a consultant to either help you develop your statement, or to tell you how to follow through. Consultants can be a very busy and expensive way of doing nothing, or of doing what you intuitively know to do anyway. The toughest part of any plan is the execution. Just do it. Eat the biggest frog first. Start by asking the right questions:

What Separates You?
Differentiate. Relative to our competitors, are we more? better? faster? cheaper? more unique? For example, the competition is keen among hotels in New Hampshire. One hotel markets to pet lovers: Put your pet order into an old New Hampshire hotel, and at check in, a rent-a-pet and litter are delivered to your room for your stay. With time-based and flexible distribution, the 7-11 product mix is changed twice daily, based on customer needs and patterns tracking. Coke

Classic's current ad consists of two dozen ads in different moods and styles for twenty different networks. Companies providing augmented and break-through products and services are positioned for the future. Do you have a(n):

a. Generic, undifferentiated product? There is nothing about what your product or service can do for customers that others cannot do. You, or it, could be replaced at any time (and, in fact, probably have by now). For example, you are a real estate agent who does no further research into properties than what is available in the MLS listings. These now are readily available to consumers. You are a professional speaker or trainer whose subject focus is Time Management. You deliver a standard program without also providing an interesting, valuable extra service or a memorable delivery. You are being replaced by interactive television training programs.

b. Is yours an *expected* product or service? For example, flights that arrive on schedule, baggage delivered intact, on-time room service, on-time delivery, accurate bank statements, pleasant greetings. Your business is declining fast.

c. Is yours an augmented 'that added extra' product? For example, at MidWest Express, every coach ticket is augmented with first class seating with lobster and shrimp. A hotel room welcomes a standard-room visitor with an in-room basket (I am writing this sentence from the Crowne Plaza at Hilton Head, SC, where my standard room came with four bottles of spring water and a bag of coated pecans—just different enough that I noticed). Your business will survive for a short while, but is vulnerable to those with break-through products or service.

d. Is yours a break-through product or service?
Nippon Telegraph & Telephone Public Corporation developed a toilet that not only generates information on blood pressure, pulse, temperature, urine, and weight, but also processes, stores, and transmits it. The information can be

viewed on a liquid crystal display, which can be located on the unit or on a nearby wall or shelf. The toilet stores up to 130 days' worth of readings, prints them out, transfers them to a personal computer, or transmits them via modem to a medical service for further analysis. Costing $7,400 it will enter the home market as the price drops. Then it will probably be able to differentiate one user's "seatprint" from another's. American Standard, introduced a smart bathtub in which the bather selects the temperature, humidity, music, air, and water flow. It's communications linkage lets you contact the tub from a remote location to ask it to have the right environment ready at a certain hour.

At the Marriott Rivercenter in San Antonio, I was door greeted by a guest services representative who followed me through the bell desk, front desk, and to my room, and handled requests for special services. Also at Marriott, the kitchens contain computers that control all functions, so that delivery to guest rooms is to-the-minute. Those are breakthrough services. Loblaws, with their experience with private branding and success with President's Choice, won a large 1992 contract as a supplier to Wal-Mart because they helped Wal-Mart develop 600 of their own in-house private label brands..

 The following ten questions are good monthly reviews:

1. What business should we be in?
2. Why do we exist? What purpose do we serve?
3. What's unique or distinctive about us?
4. Who are our principle customers, users, or clients?
5. What are our principal products, services, present and   future?
6. What are our principal markets, present and future?
7. What are our principal sources of business, present and future?
8. What is different about our business from three years ago?
9. What's likely to be different three years from now?
10. What trends are impacting our business–how are we adjusting ?

Although the setting of your mission is beyond the scope of this book, here is a beginning checklist to jump start your work:

1. Enlarge your Present Scope.

Don't just sell your product or service, *create a world*. What end result do you see if everyone used your product service in an ultimate way? Your mission statement should not read "We sell.... " but should create a vision of what will happen when your world has been created. At Motorola, Robert Galvin established a strategic intent to create a 'world of wireless communication.' That goal commitment liberated Motorola to create breakthrough products. Colgate Palmolive Chairman Reuben Mark committed Colgate to become synonymous with oral care in the customer's mind. Within two years, Colgate moved from #3 to #1. Kodak Company Chair and CEO Kay Whitmore's conceptual shift from businesses and product lines to core competencies, allowed Kodak to expand focus from film to imaging and led to new product concepts like Photo CD's.

    Write your enlarged scope here.

---

2. Re-Clarify Your Identity. Play to your long suit, your passion. Write down one strength. Don't judge it. If you don't know a strength, what is the one strength you have that people keep telling you about? Start there, because if it's perceivable, it's real.

What benefit do people get from what you do?

The seller determines the price,
but the buyer determines the value.

Be clear about what you do, and then do it. Build on it. Obsess on your strengths. Over-use them until they grow. Don't get lost. Sears got lost among Dean Whittier, Allstate and Coldwell Banker. Canadian Tire lost its focus and got lost among video discs and coffee.

 1. Write down one strength of your department and/or your company here.

_____

_____

 2.What benefit do people get from what you do?

_____

_____

_____

3. Be Flexible.
When you are sitting around envisioning the future, rewrite your mission according to the various scenarios you create. This exercise boosts confidence that even though your current mission might change if your business switches track, you'll have a new mission to guide you through.

Be able to convert, alter, enlarge or contract all your plans. Build in an escape clause. Southwest Airline's orders for sixty 737's are all convertible. AT&T modernized their Dallas plant to allow flexible manufacturing. Assume that your mission statement will change several times as you experience results. TRW started as a machine part manufacturer, and now generates profits through checking credit histories. The National Basketball Association used to make money through ticket sales, and now creates the majority of its profits through licensing and other side businesses.

4. Simplify.

Ford Motors sold almost as many cars in 1992 as 1982, with half as many workers. The Ford Taurus has only ten bumper parts; G.M.'s Grand Prix has one hundred. Southwest Airlines has a simple point-to-point route system; others have complex hub-and-spoke system routing. The 3,200 electric utilities in the United States waste billions of dollars in redundant systems and are vulnerable to small, fast-moving competitors. Apple Computer waited far too long before their 1996 cut of their product lines from over forty, to a more manageable twenty products.

Spend 80% of your time on the 20% that gives you 80% of your income. Spend 10% of your time on what does not provide income now, but will give you income in the future.

Simplify all work processes, all steps, and all procedures. Ask: "How can we make this easier?"

5. Eliminate Decay.

Have regular meetings in which you ask yourselves: Why do we do this? Hold Dumb Rules contests–employees compete for the most disrespected rules. "Dumb things we do around here that don't make any more sense." Torrance California-based Hughes Federal Credit Union held such a contest, received over 400 suggestions and implemented many of those, saving thousands of dollars.

Don't let old style human resources (HR) departments attack the company's new entrepreneurial spirit and forward motion with red tape. HR departments need to give up old notions about personnel practices: one, that fairness equals consistency, and, second, that consistency must be achieved through centralized control. Both keep companies from developing a work force that is adaptable and comfortable with ambiguity, two competencies that are critical today.

Dumb Rules:

_____

_____

_____

> *What am I doing?*
> *Why am I doing it?*
> *Am I making this more efficient when*
> *I shouldn't be doing it at all?*

How to Implement a Vision Statement

1. Give the opportunity for everyone to contribute. *Everyone.* Review their suggestions and give feedback on all of them, and why or why not they can be implemented. There is nothing more demoralizing than asking employees for suggestions and information, and then ignoring them when received.

2. Spend no longer than 45-60 days developing your statement. Companies have gone out of business putting statements together. Marriott International Inc. assigned 70 full-time staff to the job. Every Marriott hotel has a different statement, and they still have trouble implementing it.

3. Keep them short, no longer than four values. One Canadian utility passed out a folder with 36 values! If every employee cannot memorize it easily and more importantly, make all decisions by it, it doesn't work.

4. Let each department write its own as long as it fits in to the main company statement conceptually. Each department in the Ritz-Carlton group has it's own statement, but they all tie into Ritz-Carlton's overall statement.

5. Check that operations are set up to allow the statements to work.

6. Move fast! Correct as you go. You cannot have all the

details worked out if there is no time. Open up, reveal, inform constantly. Tell your people the truth as much as is possible at each stage. Start change where you will experience success and go for the early win.

Mergers and Downsizing

As you set your course, the decision to merge or downsize will most probably emerge. Although the decision to merge or downsize is outside the scope of this book, the remainder of this chapter may guide you toward more common-sense decision-making in these areas.

Companies don't make the most of new opportunities because they're making the most of old ones.

Some folks are still operating as if they were still in Stages One or Two below. The time to move into Stage Three is here. It's time to begin to concentrate on the simplicity of our central businesses, or, to get back to basics.

STAGES OF GROWTH

STAGE ONE
DO MORE WITH MORE
Until 1993
Unlimited access to funding
Growth for size
Increased mergers/acquisitions

STAGE TWO
DO MORE WITH LESS
1994-1996
Limited access to funding
Downsizing for survival
More productivity with less technical and labor costs
Frenzied merger/acquisitions

STAGE THREE
DO LESS WITH LESS
1997-8 and beyond
Marginal access to funding
Right-sizing for profit
Decrease merger/acquisitions
Non-profitable mergers and acquisitions sold off
Concentration on the simplicity of central business
Back to basics

*Those who cannot remember the past
are condemned to repeat it.*
George Satayana

Mergers and downsizing will be recorded as two of the most painful social phenomena of our decade. Some aspects of coping with these phenomena are given here because of the widespread and devastating nature of the effects of both, when poorly guided.

Mergers

Since 1991, more than 12,000 US corporations and companies have changed ownership. The 100 largest mergers have affected 4.5 million workers. In the first nine months of 1995, the value of all announced mergers reached $248.5 billion, surpassing the record full-year volume of $246.9 billion for 1988. Leading the pack were banks, health-care providers, computer-software, media, communications, entertainment, and more recently, the utility and insurance industries.

A 1995 Industry Week poll of 800 managers on the effects of buyouts and takeovers, revealed that 66% said mergers hurt morale; 85% said only shareholders and top managers were beneficiaries; 15% said that employees benefited; 20% said efficiency improved; and 50% said efficiency suffered.

One reason for this may be that most companies don't have the experience to make acquisitions, and lack follow through (Bastien, 1987). The successful part of the merger happens after the deal is signed, by combining corporate cultures and bureaucracies–a delicate and difficult venture.

Health care is not immune. Physicians, hospitals and insurance companies are turning into 'Medical Service Companies.' Many follow consultant's advice into needless and excessive mergers. Not all mergers can work, and those that do are extremely expensive in people costs.

Why Mergers Don't Always Work

1. Inadequate due diligence by acquirer or merger partner.
2. Lack of a compelling long term strategic rationale.
3. Unrealistic expectations of possible product or service synergies.
4. Paying too much up front, and underestimating the financing for the road ahead.
5. Conflicting corporate cultures.
6. Failure to move quickly to meld the two companies after the deal is complete.

Instead of a merger, consider setting up joint ventures, cooperative relationships, or joint use of equipment. Employ economies of scale–develop similar record keeping, billing and computer services to reduce paper flow. Ask your staff what to cut. Walk down to Environmental Services, the kitchen, and Maintenance and ask them how they would suggest saving money. They'll tell you.

Maintain Cultures

Before you change the character of your merged partner, recall the fate of USAIR after it painted the happy face off the Pacific Southwest Airlines (PSA) fuselage. Even though PSA was in some difficulty, it was the darling of the California traveler. When USAIR acquired it, it lost its fun commuter flair, free champagne, and ridership dropped to the current low 3.23% of San Diego's departures. Maintain as much as you can of the acquired culture.

Downsizing

In the past fifteen years one big American company after another has done this--among them IBM, Sears, GM, AT&T, and Bell Canada. Each first announced that laying off 10,000 or 20,000 or even 50,000 people would lead to an immediate turnaround. A year later there had, of course, been no turnaround, and the company laid off another 10,000 or 20,000 or 50,000–again without results. In many, if not most cases, downsizing has turned out to be something that surgeons for

centuries have warned against: 'amputation before diagnosis.'
The result is always a casualty.

Nothing can protect the worker and nobody is immune.
In fact, the more people feel protected,
the more they may be at danger.

According to a 1995 Wyatt Survey of 1,005 companies, layoffs create a downward spiral that can boost financial results
in the short term, but create a need for multiple, successive
layoffs to maintain those results. Like organizational anorex-
ia, it begins depleting the business of its fat, then its muscle,
and finally its brainpower. Layoffs emerge as a risky, painful
and inhumane form of management that only in the worst
cases can resuscitate a dying organization.

A company that experiences a layoff staggers from the loss of
talent, knowledge and morale for months, even years. The
loss of productivity after a layoff is profound. Not only does
the company lose needed employees, it can also lose customers. Layoffs may destroy consumer confidence, and that
causes the overall economy to stagnate.

A series of studies conducted by the American Management
Association (AMA) concluded that two words sum up the
ineffectiveness of layoffs: poor management. They found that
few companies engaged in long-range planning before a layoff. In a 1994 AMA study, two-thirds of the companies that
laid off, also reported hiring new employees in other areas.
Results of a 1996 Challenger, Gray, & Christmas survey
showed that Sears, AT&T, Boeing and Xerox alone have laid
off 249,836 employees since 1983. Those firms will hire
46,000 people in 1996, or 18% of the numbers they have
fired.This cycle that perpetuates and feeds itself is a very
expensive process. Dow Chemical estimates that the cost of
re-hiring a single technical or managerial employee is as much
as $50,000. Eastman Kodak began to layoff in 1985 and

since then, has restructured five times. The results are halved profit margins, a less than desirable stock price, and total revenues that aren't much larger than before they fell into the restructuring black hole.

Layoffs may have become the change tactic of choice for several reasons. Downs (1995) calls it 'mass performance management.' Executives see it as a quick way to purge the organization of those who are not pulling their weight. By creating an environment of fear, executives hope to scare employees into working harder. The message may be phrased; "the bar has been raised," "we're pushing the needle around here" or "nothing short of excellence." When combined with a layoff, it is a strong and fear-inducing method of managing employee performance. It doesn't work.

People may be fighting 'survivors guilt,' loss of co-workers, the burden of additional responsibility, and the fear of not being able to cope with increased demands. A worker might feel guilt if he is not cut, but a coworker was. Employees may mourn the loss or death of the company as they knew it. Right Associates found 74% of employees had lower morale, feared future cutbacks and distrusted management after major changes, especially after downsizing. Many functions simply cannot continue without all the necessary players in place. It still takes four musicians and four instruments to play a musical quartet. The measured productivity of nurses, teachers and social workers may diminish because many important pieces of their work are missing.

Reductions in workforce don't necessarily produce an efficient or 'lean' company. From a 1995 *The Change Letter* survey of successful corporations, these five characteristics emerged:

1. They reduced from about twelve layers of management to between four and six layers.

2. Span of control ranged from 1:10 to 1:30, up from as low

as four or five employees. They found that side benefits to increasing span were that managers had to 'manage' less and delegate more.

3. Downsizing was accompanied by a 25-50% reduction in tasks required. They found that cutting jobs without work cut-downs caused psychological reactance; employees cut down on their own.

4. Smaller operating units or profit centers (around 500 employees) were created, with the freedom to make their own decisions—as long as they were in line with company policy.

5. The greatest number of layoffs took place at corporate headquarters, since it's often the most over-staffed, most removed from customers, thus least valuable.

There have been a few admirable companies such as General Electric, and a few hospitals such as Beth Israel in Boston and Sunnybrook Hospital in Toronto, that have re-thought themselves. Instead of downsizing, they knew that the way to control costs was not to reduce expenditures, but to identify activities that are productive, that should be strengthened, promoted, and expanded.

Downsizing Guidelines

DO

1. Establish teams to identify how to distribute new work load and to avoid duplicate responsibilities and activities.

2. Get opinions, reactions, and suggestions from employees on how to handle change. If you don't act on them, explain why. And always—consult first with frontline supervisors.

3. Be careful about timing when establishing short and long term responsibilities, rewards and goals. Don't cluster events

too closely together, or people will assume they are connected. e.g. if a new CEO comes in November, wait for layoffs until a few months have passed (assuming the CEO is wise enough not to make this his or her first act). Don't make announcements at the anniversary of a massive layoff.
4. Keep upper management visible and talking, even though they are very busy. Their reassurances and accessibility are critical to a smooth transition.

DON'T

1. Don't shrink the company with general edicts about fixed across the board reductions, such as 10% from every department.

2. Don't cut out jobs but keep the bureaucracy intact. Assess each department and identify extraneous expenses and their cuts.

3. Don't cut employees and maintain the same work level expectations. People will become overburdened, resentful, and exhausted.

4. Don't make impulsive, poorly conceived changes. They add to an atmosphere of unpredictability. Think through consequences. Use a scalpel, not a meat cleaver.

5. Don't keep people in the dark. Employees want answers to questions such as: "How stable are we as a company? Who is in control? Who is in charge of operations? Is my job in danger? What am I supposed to do?"

6. Don't stress the short term only. Have prepared answers to the following questions: "What will happen after new people arrive, procedures are written, and employees move?"

Alternatives to Downsizing

Dow Chemical held off a hiring binge even when business was booming to avoid an eventual layoff. According to Dow's figures, laying off a manager can cost anywhere from $30,000 to $100,000 or more.

Layoffs are horribly
expensive and destructive of shareholder value.
Frank Popoff, CEO, 3M

When 3M's net income dropped twelve percent, the company began making some major changes, but not mass firing. Hewlett-Packard has handled unneeded employees through its internal 'excess' program, and by offering voluntary severance packages. The excess program boasts a high rate of placement of extra employees into other jobs in the company

Alternatives to Downsizing

Cut salaries temporarily
Intel chose progressive
salary cuts according to paycheck size,
with the lowest checks receiving no cuts.

Layoff rotations

Shortened work week

Flexible employment

Early retirement. Northwest gave lump sums of
$20,000. This is an expensive option,
and often the best workers go.

Delay projects

Create revenue generating tasks for all employees
Don't cost-cut your way out of a revenue problem.

and can include retraining.

 Look back over the notes you've made in the margins in this chapter. Condense them into two action points; two changes you will make as a result of reading this section.

Actions I will take:

1._____

2._____

Chapter Three
Jump Starting Change

There is nothing more difficult to take in hand, more per-
ilous to conduct, or more uncertain in its success, than to
take the lead in the introduction of a new order of things.
Niccolo Machiavelli

Your present organization is a poor predictor of the kinds of changes you will need to make. Your not-yet-existing business is the best source of information for what the future organization should look like.

So instead of remodeling what you have, understand what it will take to run that future business. Compare the future organization with the one you have now, and initiate a plan to get you from here to there based on the future, not on the present. The best place to look is in the future business, and the worst place to look is in the current organization.

Your future business was one you established in Chapter Two, 'Setting Your Course.' So, now that it's set, consider starting the change process:

Beginning the change process

1. Tell the Truth.

Someone has to tell the organization the truth, usually someone from the outside who has not absorbed the corporate mindset. Hire consultants who are not afraid to lose their contracts; that is, who are willing to tell the company the truth about itself.

2. See the pattern.

Acknowledge the pattern of corporate crisis. Make it clear to everyone that the company is in crisis not because people have damaged it, but because good practices have outlasted their useful lives. There is no blame. Acknowledge the value of the past. If you know that what has gone before wasn't wasted or thrown out, you can give it up more easily. The sense of loss is less. Some companies throw parties to honor the past; at Honeywell, they held a mock wake to mark the closing of a plant. Everybody talked, cried, said good-bye, and then were able to go on. Hold a clear act, or rite of passage, to indicate that the past is gone.

3. Examine Origins.

Examine the founder's vision, the good reasons for the vision, what mechanisms were put in place to carry it out, and how much of that vision still works. The originator of the organization reflected the needs of the time; there is no disloyalty in abandoning practices that no longer serve present needs.

The company needs to change not because people have outlasted their usefulness, but because of new demands placed upon us.

4. Examine current beliefs.

Find out the company's beliefs, or what makes up the 'unconscious' or buried principles of strategy. To do this, examine how managers act with customers, suppliers, employees, and

> What things did we do in order to get into the crisis we now face?
>
> What was our founder's vision, and what did he put in place to make it come to life, day after day, year after year? Does that vision still work?
>
> What is the company really thinking, the company's unconscious? What are the buried principles of strategy enacted in what managers routinely do with customers, suppliers, employees, and each other?
>
> Look in detail at what the company does.

each other, and then explore the logic underlying those behaviors. Examine metaphors, myths, humor, and cartoons. Chapter Seven gives guidance on uncovering and changing a company's belief system.

5. Broadcast the results.
Lay out the evidence for everyone to see, let people talk it over and come back with questions and disbeliefs. Sharing information is crucial during all stages of change, but especially as the change process is beginning.

6. Create your Vision or Mission –see Chapter Two.

7. Tell people what is going to happen.
Even if the news is unpleasant, tell people early and allow time for the news to sink in. Suggest ways they can prepare by reading or developing new skills. But don't slide or turbocharge your way through the past because of the discomfort in grieving it. As soon as you know that a change is on the horizon, explain to your people why change is happening, the planned sequence of events, how and who will implement what, who will be affected, and how the company and operations will differ. Even when you don't know the whole picture, give what information you have and clearly tell your

people the parts you don't know.

Research on pre-op patients showed that those who were fully informed handled surgery better, and had a better post-operative course. Stanley Schacter's (1962) studies on the effects of giving information, misinformation and no information under stress conditions showed that those subjects who were injected with epinephrine (which produces symptoms associated with anxiety such as rapid heart beat, pulse, sweating or a 'stress condition') reacted differently depending on

---

Beginning the Change Process

1. Honor the Past. Acknowledge value of the past. If people know what has gone before wasn't wasted or thrown out, they can give it up more easily; the sense of loss is less. Tell people what's going to happen even if unpleasant and allow time for the news to sink in. Suggest ways they can prepare by developing new skills.

2. Keep information flowing out. People in denial need information. A small part of them needs to know. Feed this part with meetings, notices, videos. Explain why change is happening, the sequence of events, how and who will implement it, who will be affected, and how the company and operations will differ. Even when you don't know the whole picture, give what information you have. It's perfectly acceptable to tell them you don't know.

---

information received and environmental cues. Those who received no information shaped their behavior according to what they perceived in their environment; and those who were informed, attributed anxiety to the drug. Keep information flowing out.

Keep your personal appearance high.
Michael Blumenthal, former CEO, Unisys

How to Communicate Change
Watson Wyatt Worldwide in 1993 investigated 531 United States organizations undergoing major restructuring. The

question: "If you could go back and change one thing, what would it be?" The most frequent answer: "The way I communicated with my employees." Frontline supervisors, not senior managers, are the opinion leaders in your organization (Strebel, 1996).

Communicate facts, not values.
Communicate face-to-face.
Don't count on on videos, publications, or large meetings.
Target frontline supervisors. Do not let executives introduce the change to frontline employees.

The only effective way to communicate a value is to act in accordance with it and give others the incentive to do the same.

Align Behavior and Reward
If you value customer service, then recruitment, performance appraisals, promotions, and bonuses should be based on customer service performance. Create objective measures for performance that are important to you. Live the values, act the deeds. According to Wyatt (1993), 68% of large companies consider missions and values to be their number one communication priority. Sadly, they attempt to get these across directly. What is true for people is true for organizations. Seventy percent of the major companies in a 1992 Jensen Group survey, had revised their corporate missions during recent restructuring. Only nine percent felt that revising their missions helped them achieve the objectives of the restructuring.

When Acts do not Support Values
According to Mirvis and Kanter (1989), 43% of employees believe that management cheats and lies, and the frontline is the most cynical group of all. A 1994 study by the Council of Communication Management shows that 64% of employees believe that management is often lying. *The Wall Street*

Journal reported that two-thirds of senior personnel managers surveyed by Right Associates said that employees trust management less after a restructuring (*WSJ*, 11/2/92).

Employees will infer what you value from your behavior. They will adopt your values only if they are convinced that those values will enable them to attain their personal goals. Propaganda won't help.

A large paper manufacturing company in the mid-west was undergoing major change. Thousands of employees watched senior managers unveil a new mission. The slogan Teamwork Together Tomorrow was on a gigantic video screen behind the speaker's platform. Employees received duffle bags, caps, and coffee mugs inscribed with the three T's. When they returned to work, however, they found a letter from the union accusing the company of hiring private investigators to watch employees suspected of stealing, using drugs, and making fraudulent disability claims.

Say in the fewest words possible what you plan to do. Put the facts down on paper. This will guide communication between senior managers and supervisors, and between supervisors and frontline employees.

In periods of high stress and uncertainty, people fill communication voids with rumors; rumors end up attributing the worst possible motives to those in control. Any communication lowers employees' stress and anxiety even when the news is bad. Uncertainty is more painful than bad news. Keep information flowing out. People need about tenfold the amount of information you think they do.

Keep all information short, simple, clear and interesting. People won't read more than seven seconds if they are not highly motivated and/or their interest has not been piqued.

Start a reverse flow of information, so that the flow becomes bi-directional. If your change is too complicated to communicate simply, then simplify the change. The limits of what you can communicate as facts are the limits of what you can do.

a. Cut out every unnecessary word.
b. Avoid management proclamations.
c. Tell employees, straight up, exactly what you plan to do.
d. Don't lie, fudge or hide.
e. Don't worry about employees leaking information to your competitors. Your competitors already know. Hackers can infiltrate your most secure material in minutes. Besides, if all you can do is track your competitors, you're in poor competitive shape.

Communicate Face-to-Face
The best way to communicate a major change to the frontline workforce is face-to-face. Do not use videos or video hookups, do not introduce the change in a company publication, and do not hold large meetings with frontline employees. Video has been the fastest-growing medium for communicating with employees even though evidence is that employees don't watch videos. Video ranks eleventh out of 14 communication methods, according to studies conducted jointly by the IABC (International Association of Business Communicators) and by Towers Perrin (1984). Sixty percent of large British companies have used videos to communicate major change, according to a 1993 study by the Institute of Management, a British trade association, yet 75% of those companies believe that the videos are ineffective.

Group vs. Individual Communication. Don't gather people into groups. When frontline employees are anticipate major change, the last thing you should do is gather them into a large group. The group mentality is unpredictable.

Publications and Newsletters. Publications are perceived as untrustworthy and are often incomprehensible (Larkin & Larkin, 1996). In the midst of major change in the early 1990's, Whirlpool asked its employees to evaluate the company publication, *Vision*. Only 20% thought that the publication was "valuable and believable (Moore, 1994). A 1992 study by Mercer Management Consulting of 200 employee communication managers, showed that 70% referred to their publications as "attempts at the truth," and less than 15% said that the publications reflected the entire truth. People don't read your newsletters because the information in every article has been screened, pruned, softened, toned down, and hyped up.

When a change requires frontline employees to do their jobs differently, give the information face-to-face, first in discussions between senior managers and frontline supervisors, and then between supervisors and their frontline staff. The experts are the frontline supervisors, the people who communicate with frontline employees daily. Workers are reasonable and cooperative as individuals but in groups, a different mind-set prevails.

Corporate videos, publications, and meetings don't move information through companies; they inhibit it. The most effective way to communicate is informally, face-to-face, one-on-one. No matter what the change–merger, restructuring, downsizing, reengineering, the introduction of new technology, or a customer service campaign–the first words frontline employees hear about a change should come from their supervisor. Employees would rather receive information from their immediate supervisors than from senior managers.

What to Do

1. Arrange a meeting with one senior manager and eight to ten supervisors.

2. Bring a single piece of paper outlining the changes needed,

for each person. Divide this into two parts: willing to change, and not willing to change. Create a response system that signals clearly whether the supervisor is on board and committed (green card), cautious (yellow card), or unwilling to accept the change (red card). A supervisor who holds up a red card has an additional responsibility: to state why he/she is opposed to the change, and what suggestions he/she would make to overcome the problem.

3. Describe items in the not-willing to change column; request recommendations for items in the willing-to change column.

4. Never give away the power to decide. Make it clear that power to decide *what* to do remains with the senior management change team. Decisions on *how* to make the changes can rest with supervisors and employees.

5. Keep meetings shorter than 90 minutes.

The traditional approach is to launch change from the top and hope that communication about the change will spread like wildfire. But frontline supervisors are the opinion leaders in your organization. Because frontline supervisors greatly influence the attitudes and behaviors of others, they are critical to the success of any change effort. Ameritech, AT&T, Cadbury Schweppes, Exxon Chemical, GE, General Tire, GM, Hewlett-Packard, and Santa Fe have all found that the immediate supervisor is the preferred source of information. Spend 80% of your communication time, money, and effort on supervisors.

Allan is a maintenance supervisor at a western Canadian ski resort. Allan's department has the least downtime, the fewest discipline problems, the lowest rate of absenteeism, and the best safety record in the company. It's not because he has the 'easiest' people in the company. It's because he has earned the respect and loyalty of his employees. One afternoon, after the lifts closed, three hundred ski resort workers gathered in the cafeteria. Under a banner that read *Ski 2000: Eagle's Mountain*, senior managers announced changes.

Allan heard for the first time that the ski resort would no longer have supervisors. Supervisors would become CFs (change facilitators). Allan's maintenance department would become a CAT (change action team). Every frontline employee would be empowered to submit CAOs (change action opportunities). Allan was told that he would be helped with the cultural transition: Professors from the University of British Columbia would run courses to help him 'evolve' from a 'boss' into a facilitator of his CAT's CAOs. Allan's hair stood on end. He has lost the respect of his workers. Allan would have been more likely to help his workers to accept change, if the company had treated him as a vital source of information and as an opinion leader. As it was, Allan had no choice but to sabotage. And he did.

Employees will change the way they go about their jobs only if they learn about what is expected of them from a familiar and credible source. Communication between frontline supervisors and employees counts the most toward changed behavior where it matters the most: at the front line.

Push planning and control of profits down to product lines.

Avoid building up headquarters staffs.

Open up communication channels so that competitive and financial information flows down to the shop floor, and suggestions flow up to the chairman.

It sounds easy, but making a big company more flexible, requires a complete change in how people act and think, to move away from a large centralized organization.
Emerson CEO Charles F. Knight

Hold small focus groups of workers who have immediate contact with their jobs to determine what problems they have, what their needs are, and what suggestions they have for the company.

Communicate these needs in such a way as they are heard, through frontline supervisors, progressively up through the layers of the organization, with minimal system delay. Follow information manually to analyze delays and unblock them.

Act on these needs and suggestions where possible, flowing information back down in response to them with minimal system delay. Follow information manually to analyze blocks and delays.

Begin 360 degree evaluation. Employees evaluate their immediate supervisors and peers. Feedback sessions should be supervised.

Reach agreements on the common vision and common goals of the unit. Assess authority and responsibility at each level, and create open agreement regarding levels of delegation. Create a values outline whereby decisions can be made.

Strengthen those actions in the best interests of the company, and weaken purely self-serving actions. Challenge 'look good' or other symptomatic solutions. Monitor and correct each of the symptoms which creates a non-productive atmosphere.

Choose the start of change carefully

Start in the unit or department where there is some leverage. That is, start change with the unit or line that holds a place of enough relevance in the company that if there is turnaround, it will influence the other units in a positive way. Start where there is an openness and willingness to participate. That is, most people in the unit are committed to change, and to permitting intrusion by an outside source to help with change.

Start where there is an adequate burden of responsibility, or lack of blame shift. Most of the members of the unit indicate that they are responsible for their own outcomes, and relatively few have burned out or have become apathetic.

Start where changes will be manageable. There should also be few enough reporting layers that a reversal of present practices or of the change process does not become unwieldy.

Ask the People Who Do the Work *How* to Change

The people who know the work best are the ones who perform it. In a 1995 $20 million plane repainting error, United Airlines' hired a research firm to consumer-test colors, ignoring staff and pilots' advice. Weekly newspapers, company-wide meetings, e-mail, and an in-house TV show keep people up-to-date. They make decisions quickly, and with a flat approval tree.

The highly skilled clerks at Home Depot have the time and patience to expertly guide customers. Even according to David Glass, CEO of Wal-Mart, Home Depot runs the best retail organization in America. Typical shoppers spend only $38 per visit but return 30 times a year. Why does your author keep coming back? Not just because the setting reminds me of the time I spent in my father's workshop. No, because of Home Depot's Ken Langone's 'anything-we-can-do-to-make-the-store-better, just-let-us-know' attitude. Home Depot's outside directors must visit twelve stores per quarter, instead of holding stuffy quarterly meetings in paneled boardrooms. How do store-level employees come up with 70-80% of business improvements? They are asked.

The single most important strategy for success during rapid change, rated #1 by Gault from Goodyear, Walsh from Tenneco, and Allaire at Xerox, is to ask employees the following: "If you were the CEO of this company, how would you run it?" Often those guarding the best information, and the least likely asked, are the administrative assistant staff.

List everyone that could be affected by your changes and decisions. Use the RACI (Responsibility, Authority, Control, Influence) model: Who is responsible for this change, who will have authority over this changes, who has control and who can influence it?

R	Who is responsible for this?
A	Who has authority over it?
C	Who has had control over this in the past?
I	Who else is influenced by it?

Get everyone to buy into the system. Change stops at the level that doesn't buy in. Thus, if a Vice-President is change resistant, everything below her won't work. People cue in on their immediate leader.

> *The revolution we started has gone at best, only halfway.*
> *I have learned that half a revolution is not better than none.*
> *In fact, it may be worse.*
> Jim Champy

Change All at Once

Revise research and development, manufacturing, information systems, people systems, and finance carefully, then change them all at once. IBM and GM are cutting costs and closing plants without changing other systems. Xerox, on the other hand, is changing design cycles, improving quality, empowering workers, reducing their supplier base, and improving relationships with remaining suppliers. All parts have to move together and be economically aligned.

Make sure all systems are aligned. AT&T, General Electric, Johnson & Johnson and UPS have thrived with decentralization due to strong leadership and quick response to external forces. On the other hand, PepsiCo's Kentucky Fried Chicken decentralized during a quality-improvement drive two years ago, but ended up with a bureaucratic mess.

McDonnell Douglas Corporation, Avery Dennison, and

> ### MIT's Change Recipe
>
> ❏ Do simple things first.
> ❏ Learn to do them flawlessly.
> ❏ Add new layers of activity over results of simple tasks.
> ❏ Don't change the simple things.
> ❏ Make the new layer work as flawlessly as predecessor.
> ❏ Repeat 1-5 endlessly.

General Dynamics are among corporations recentralizing. Bill Eaton, Senior VP at Levi-Strauss says, "It shows you how important a decision to move in one direction can be. Getting back together again is harder than splitting up."

Senior-Level Change

A senior-level management change deserves special attention because it creates effects that can run wide and deep. Left unattended, these changes can divide an organization quickly. With a senior-level management change, the leader faces learning a new environment, a new business, and new players, as well as resistance, anxiety, and competition among both subordinates and peers. Enduring impressions of, and by, the leader, are formed during the first 90 days. Miscues can be costly and lasting. To give staff the opportunity to get to know the senior executive in a short period of time, and to build relationships quickly, try the following:

1. Appoint a facilitator who is trusted by employees.
2. Have the facilitator hold a single meeting with direct reports, and a general meeting with the whole organization to answer questions. Why was the leader selected? What does she bring to the company? What is her style? How does she perform, communicate.
3. The facilitator asks employees to identify the problems the new manager will face in the next six to twelve months. How would employees solve them? What do they want most from

her? How do they see themselves as a working group, and what do they want the new manager to know about them?
4. The facilitator then reports the findings to the leader and discusses her response.

> ## Jump Starting Change
>
> **What to Do**
> 1. Show empathy and understanding.
> 2. Encourage sharing of ideas and suggestions for moving on.
> 3. Clarify perceived loss, real wants, and what is happening.
> 4. Share purpose of change; connect old and new methods.
> 5. Engage a commitment to change
>
> **For All Changes**
> 1. Hold ceremonies and create symbols.
> 2. Take ownership of change, vision, commitment, and alignment of purpose.

Summary

Move fast! Correct as you go. You cannot have all the details worked out if there is no time.

Open up, reveal, inform constantly. Tell your people the truth as much as is possible at each stage.

Start change where you will experience success and go for the early win.

Most importantly, take action. Don't fail by the FBI Syndrome, 'Failure by Indecision.'

Do it. Do anything, correct as you go. The worst thing you can do is nothing. At least when you're moving, you're learning.

> *If you come to a fork in the road, take it.*
> Yogi Berra

Look back over the notes you've made in the margins in this chapter. Condense them into two action points; two changes you will make as a result of reading this section.

Actions I will take:

1._____

2._____

Chapter Four
The Infomated Customer

*Ozzie and Harriet don't live here any more;
in fact, they don't live anywhere.*

The shift from capital toward knowledge means that the knowledge base can shift anywhere, and this is one of the greatest competitive challenges for North American business. The share of Ph.D. recipients from Taiwan remaining in the United States after graduation fell from 53% in 1980 to 32 percent in 1991. The share of Korean graduates remaining in the United States fell from 41 percent to 23 percent in the same period (Morrison, 1996). The knowledge base is shifting.

What will the info-organization of the future look like? What will the company do that is different than what it does today? What are change-adaptive companies doing now to position themselves for the future? How can you position yourself to compete for the infomated customer of tomorrow? This chapter will give you ideas on how companies have informationalized to stay ahead of change.

Imagine your daily life today. Take away your fax machine, your computer, your phone, your TV and your remote control. Take away zippers, washing machines, refrigerators, ball-point pens, everything plastic, pantihose, fluorescent lighting, cars, telephones, and lighting–it is now the year 1896. If product cycles were between 50 and 100 years then, and only six to 18 months now, do you think you could even begin to imagine your future? You can't. Yet it is possible to create approximations of the future based on what has already been invented.

Why will the future be different? Most old-wave computers work according to a deterministic model; they can do only what they are programmed to do, and don't do well with ambiguity or approximation. New computers will make decisions based on indeterminate inputs and will be able to intuit, judge, and emote–neural network development makes these highly possible. Financial services are seeking machines that can read handwriting accurately. Commercial bankers, underwriters, and brokers have a major interest in using neurocomputing to read handwritten numbers and verify signatures on checks and other documents. Neurocomputers predict stock prices, score credit applications, and analyze mortgage and loan applications.

Packages and processes are being developed that will give infinite shelf life to consumables. Miniaturization in the next economy might compress the big metal refrigerator to the size of a thin film that shrink-wraps directly around any food or beverage, which can then sit temperature-controlled on pantry shelves. There are cans today that may be stored at room temperature, yet instantly cool the beverage inside the moment they are opened. Smart refrigerators will monitor our intake, the way that smart toilets can now guard our health while monitoring our 'outtake.' Food, clothing, machinery, and any tangible good may be biologically monitored, maintained, and improved. By the time that the bio-economy arrives, the company that manufactures refrigera-

capture and use information at each point of contact with customers will be better off than those that do so at only one or a few points. Each point of contact can be informationalized to improve customer service and operating efficiency.

Change the way you share information.

Use internet sales, interactive video-on-demand, CD-ROM or other technology to approach customers. For the real estate trade, push the service edge by acquiring and developing a new technology to share MLS information from one set of folks (buyers) to another set (sellers). Banking and insurance professionals are becoming 'information brokers.' Investment banking is available to small business through 24-hr. videoconferencing kiosks, ATM's that trade stocks, and satellite. In the virtual banking world, customers log onto the Citibank channel, buy stocks and pay bills. Record stores sell games, comic books, computer software and greeting cards. Superstores mix concerts with cappuccino. Professional speakers are available on cable's The Peoples Network (TPN), Real Estate Television Network (RETN), among others.

Anyone who has access to customer databases can, and will, compete with you.

Leapfrog your competition by changing the way you inform. In-home systems such as TV, computers, and catalogs provide portability of time and place. Try catalogs' new distribution channels such as Catalog Cash, a combination of several catalogs supporting a frequent-buyer program introduced at nine ShopRite Supermarkets, or video catalogs in kiosks in retail stores or in malls such as Florsheim and Levi Strauss & Co.

Watch out for information exhaust that can be captured, processed, or recycled.

TV Guide is nothing more than a well-packaged listing of television broadcast schedules, information that is available to anyone from a number of sources. The Official Airlines

Guide (OAG), consolidates flight information, yet this basic concept created a business with a greater market value than all but the largest airlines. Quotron provides information about security prices to brokerage companies. It simply filled a need by capturing securities transaction information and recycling it back to the brokerage industry that generated the information in the first place.

Don't wait until independent entrepreneurs and more advanced competitors collect, process, and sell critical information generated by your core business.

Direct computerized self-reservation and ticketing provides an additional benefit: customers who design their own flight packages also build customer profiles. When you use a Citibank/American Airlines Visa card, for example, you not only earn a mile for every dollar spent, both companies build their customer data-base profile, purchase by purchase. TRW is an auto parts and aerospace company with an info-business, Information Services Group (ISG), that will dominate the firm's growth and profits. The Credit Services Division, ISG's main unit, operates a data base of 145 million records of individual credit histories and provides credit ratings. TRW wants to integrate other sources of information into their current credit-base core. By integrating demographic, family, Social Security, medical, and other data with credit histories, TRW can increase its value. By building title and data bases from public information sources, it can validate titles and issue title insurance instantly, and has the potential to offer real-time mortgage application and review services. Such services let Citicorp make a mortgage commitment within fifteen minutes, and Canada Trust in Toronto to issue loans by phone. All this can be done only by informationalizing the mortgage lending business. According to Davis & Davidson (1991) in *2020 Vision*, the value of any product can be increased by incorporating information content.

Embed information features and functions in all products. Choice, variety, and service placed into traditional products create smart products and new market opportunities.

The head of a major trucking company had the opportunity to develop an industry-wide trucking information service that matched shipping requests with trucking schedules. They refused because it would help the customer select competing carriers. What the CEO didn't get, was that controlling information is a better business than trucking. When existing industry participants neglect the information dimensions of their business, independent third parties come in to fill this role. FTD joins customers and florists. Pizzanet gathers up mom-and-pop pizza parlors to compete against home delivery pizza giants. Develop information services about all players, your competitors as well as yourself. *The Journal of Commerce* offers a service to the shipping industry called Trans-Rates which lists all schedules and rates for shipping companies. An outside party captured this business because each shipping company could not envision a service that might result in helping customers choose another carrier.

Profitability from the new features may exceed the profit from the original product or service. The more information you put into a product, or the more you are able to use a product to pull out information, the more you evolve beyond the original purpose into even far greater opportunities.

Within ten years, companies will have blended these old and new businesses, and the distinction will be more analytical than real. Winners will have shifted focus from industrial-age products, services, and channels to new info-business lines and distribution channels. The new info-businesses will include services that provide turbocharged information, industry-wide product offerings, preview, and twenty-four-hour access.

In the information economy, focus on the customer.
Build around client benefits. Show people
how to get what they want and they'll
move heaven and earth to get it.

Redefine competition.

If the game hinges on price, change the rules and redefine the basis of competition. There are many different strategies or combinations of strategy to use as your primary competitive weapon. The key is to redefine competitive strategy in the eyes of the customer. Many companies are defining themselves, and competing on the basis of, price. However, according to Burrus (*Technotrends*, 1993), price is the least effective long-term strategy. Here are some bases of competition for the future, from the least to the most effective:

Alternative Types of Competition
Price
Reputation
Image
Time
Innovation
Values
Service

Price competition is deadly. If you hold your prices steady or reduce them to expand your market share, you start eliminating resources that are vital to your organization's long-term survival. The United States airline industry comes to mind as a great example of the lose-lose nature of price competition. Almost the entire industry has been at the edge of bankruptcy since it began focus on a price-based competitive strategy, or price wars. **Reputation-based and image-based** strategies are also old standbys; IBM is an example. It effectively combined an image-based strategy with a reputation-based strategy as the central focus through the highly competitive 1980's.

Values-Based Competition

Consumers are desensitized to overstated claims. A car manufacturer says that its cars are the 'heartbeat of America,' an airline 'flies the friendly skies,' a brokerage firm is 'rock solid.' Cynicism has developed among consumers who have developed low expectations about the ability of companies to do what they say they'll do or be different from their competitors in a meaningful way. Ben & Jerry's, the Body Shop, Apple Computer, Smith & Hawken, and Starbucks Coffee are character positioners. Character companies look for situations that build pride in their organization and loyalty in customers. Howard Schultz, CEO of Starbucks, believes that the quality of his work force is the company's only sustainable competitive advantage, and that workers need to feel pride in and stake in the outcome of the labor. Anita and Gordon Roddick founded the Body Shop to sell cosmetics to achieve well-being instead of potions to fulfill fantasies of instant rejuvenation.

Build around client benefits. Show people how to get what they want, and they'll move heaven and earth to get it.

Service-Based Competition

Manage customers, not products. Service-based competition is placed at the bottom because it provides the foundation for the rest. Without it, the others are weakened. Customer-centered management is a strategic necessity. Whereas the product-driven enterprise survives only by attracting a stream of new customers for products that can be copied by a competitor almost overnight, customer-centered enterprises can find new products and services for their most loyal customers. They do this either by mass customizing, or by creating partnerships with other providers. If customers and customer information are the company's most valuable assets, then organize the firm around them—to manage customers as well as products and brands. Instead of selling a product to segments of the population, build portfolios of customers and manages the lifetime value of each.

The customer-centered firm puts every customer into one portfolio, with the manager in charge of that portfolio responsible for building customer dialogue. In your department or company, red circle the top fifteen percent of your customers who give you 60% of your business. Once you've identified your Most Valuable Customers, put a 'picket fence' around them to insulate the group from traditional marketing efforts. It's not simple to build a one to-one relationship with customers. It requires complete commitment to each customer and must be integrated across all company operations. Here are a few guides to help you on your way.

Choose your top people to manage your top customers. This way, your customer-managed business will evolve more quickly. You'll soon need to provide new products and services for these customers, and you will need the expertise of top people to serve as experts and administrators for the products you already have. Appoint customer managers to be responsible for specific customers. Draw a red circle around these customers. As your new marketing practices take hold, enlarge the circle, placing more and more customers 'under new management.' Add more dedicated customer managers, and sort your customers into better-defined portfolios.

Increase Contact Frequency. Remember the old saying "out of sight out of mind?" Now, with thousands of offers to buy every day, your clients need to hear from you at least every other week. Send congratulations, a newsletter, write articles, announce new services, promote free publications, give public seminars, write a column, send news releases, go on radio or TV talk shows. Keep clients informed about themselves and their competitors, and keep clients informed about you.

Build random call backs to your customers. Schedule three calls a week to various clients, asking, "how are we doing and how could we do it better?" Everybody in the company should call, for example, the loading dock should call to ask in what condition did your parcel arrive? Call your own business. Sit in your own waiting room. Buy your own products.

Do Business with Yourself. Sometimes customers can't express their needs or remember problems they have had with a product or service. Observe them being customers. Xerox uses anthropologists at its Palo Alto Research Center to observe users of new document products in their offices. Digital Equipment developed an interactive process called 'contextual inquiry' to watch users of new technologies. Milliken created 'first-delivery teams' that accompany the first shipment of all products. Team members follow the product through the customer's production process to see how it is used and then develop ideas for further improvement. Bill Chiles, former CEO of SuperCuts, would sit in waiting rooms to listen, observe, and intelligently track customer needs.

Question Internal and External Clients. Do a better customer survey, which may *not* mean an improved version of your standard format. In fact, your standard format may be outdated. Become more creative in the way you ask questions of your customers. The Dumb Rules contest described elsewhere in this book was a cost-effective, less painful, and profitable way to survey how employees felt about the company.

There's a big difference between what you think you're promoting and what clients think you're promoting. Make a list of all things of value you think you give customers. Rank how important you think they are. Talk to your customers and your executives, have *them* rank the same items. See the difference. Quality and service are the things your customers say they are. At Foothills Hospital in Calgary, surveys indicated that 'treating us as adults' was more important than 'getting well.' Being informed was more important than being treated by the latest in medical equipment. Check with employees quarterly as well. Ask them: "What is our mission, values, and goals?" You might find they are not what you would expect. If they are not what you expect, then the message employees are sending to customers will be mixed too.

Involve the Customer. Texonic makes sport fisherman depth finders. Because their products weren't selling well, Texonic asked folks what they wanted, and found that they wanted LCD so they could use fish finders in sunlight. Texonic went back to engineering, built it, called it 'Hummingbird,' and now it's best seller. Lexus was 'reverse engineered,' based on customer information. Toyota assembled reams of data on what upper-income consumers valued in a vehicle, and has created a buying experience in which the customer feels special and valued. IKEA evolved from a small Swedish mail-order furniture operation into the world's largest retailer of home furnishings. The key elements are not unlike others: good Scandinavian design, global sourcing, knock-down kits, easy access from suburban stores, and extras such as food, free strollers, wheelchairs, and day care. They involve customers by giving free pens, paper, tape measures, and they will lend or sell at cost, roof racks for you to take it home. IKEA mobilizes customers to do things they've never done before–their own value-creating activities.

Restaurants eat up more than food, and unless there is a high-volume banquet business, they'll eat up hotel profits too. Loew's Vanderbilt, Chicago Embassy Suites, Le Meridien and others have tried cook-your-own eateries, switching to bistros and coffee houses and found that the switch away from the standard sit-down restaurant can often mean more room nights. The real value of the cook-your-own idea is in customer involvement.

Very often consumers want the gratification that comes from feeling in control. Some factors feeding this desire for control are: advances in communications and information technology that are drastically reducing the cost of information, higher levels of education, availability of more information through expanded media, a widespread distrust of experts, and a strong consumer-advocacy movement. The nature of the consumer has changed from uninformed and passive to informed and adversarial. In effect, the consumer demands alternatives. When there aren't choices, consumers help create them by finding substitute products and services, and become willing customers for creative entrepreneurs. People want fast answers and will do-it-themselves to save money. By allowing customers to help create your product, the win-win of increased loyalty and customers feeling more in control results.

By 1997, the US Postal Service promises to charge by the amount of service needed, rather than by the four current mail classes. The new system is keyed to customers willingness to bar code and sort. IKEA furniture charges less when customers do some of their own work. Despite early bugs, self-service bar-coding and customer grocery check-out show promise in reducing costs. Boosting this trend are charge cards that keep getting smarter. A single plastic card will soon serve as airline ticket, hotel-room key, car-rental contract, telephone calling card, insurance policy and expense reporter. Some agencies' computers already maintain records of customer travel preferences, provide information on destinations, and let their customers use the system for a lower fee. The Arizona Biltmore has locks that let guests use credit cards to check in without ever going to the front desk, potentially reducing costs. Can you teach your customers to do part of the work?

Provide One-Stop Shopping
You can't invest in the Mayo clinic but you can invest in the Kahler Corporation, a hotel chain with 40% revenues from Mayo patients. The 700-room Kahler in Rochester, Minnesota has a full-time nurse, waiters who understand spe-

cial diets, and an amenity package that includes medicine cups. Carmax, Circuit City's used car lot, holds 1,000 cars, and takes care of all needs, including financing in under an hour. McDonald's is now in 700 Wal Marts, and in eighteen Home Depots, and is planning on 800 by 1998. TravelFest Superstores are one-stop shopping travel centers for visa applications, travelers checks, luggage, gadgets, with 80% of revenue from tickets and reservations. Create a reason for consumers to shop and entertain them to boot. Boston-based Continuum Care Corporation is building a West Palm $34 million Medical Mall. St. Joseph Health Center in Kansas City, Missouri, is a dry cleaner, gift shop, bank, restaurants, rehabilitation therapy, pulmonary clinic, radiology, and out-patient surgery center. Radiology services are up nine percent, and ultrasound is up by 45%. Nordstrom's department store offer mammograms to women. Serving the infomated customer means anytime, anywhere, anyhow.

This is your own business. Do your own thing.
Don't listen to us in Seattle. Listen to your customer.
James Nordstrom.

In summary:
Infomate your business *and* your customer's business.
Build everything around your customer's needs.
Capture the information exhaust from your own business.
Compete on service, not price.
Involve the customer in your product or service.

 Look back over the notes you've made in the margins in this chapter. Condense them into two action points; two changes you will make as a result of reading this section.

Actions I will take:

1._____

2._____

Chapter Five
Getting Fast and Flexible

Management today has to think like a fighter pilot. When things move so fast, you can't always make the right decision —so you have to learn to adjust, to correct more quickly.

What will the company of the future look like? What will companies do that is different than what they do today? What are change-adaptive companies doing now to position themselves for the future? Top companies are getting fast and flexible. Chapter Five examines what can be done to increase speed and flexibility in *your* company.

Move Faster

We have become a people who gas up at credit card pumps to save less than three minutes, and who punch 'two minutes' into our microwaves, and become impatient with the wait. Business has responded. Using a pen computer with an electromagnetic stylus for data entry, hotel vans notify the front desk, so that guests are not only checked in when they arrive, the lights and radio are remotely turned on in their rooms. At Designs Inc., (Levi-Strauss), information technology has eliminated not only central warehousing, but also overstocking and running short. Operating with 33% the overhead of any chain of it size in the United States, each day the 500 stores at Mrs. Fields Cookies get a customized sales plan from corporate.

Build fast reaction into your customer response loop.
Order from PC Connection before 3:00 AM on the east coast, and receive delivery the same day. Domino's partially prepares pizzas, and then finishes them off when a customer order comes in. New flash-bake technology lets pizzas be baked in the van on the way to a customer, cutting even more time off the order. Roger Kao of the Golden WOK benchmarked Domino's, then increased speed and sales even more by storing delivery address and directions by phone number. New customer orders are compared with old ones to increase upselling. Orders are automatically routed to the closest location and at the location, to the right work station, all of which have their own PC's. Medstations, or ATM's for drugs, are getting high ratings from nursing staffs. Instead of charts, checking, keys, cabinets, recording, inventories, thefts, and wasted time, the Medstation needs only an ID, password, and name. Only the selected drug appears, which is automatically inventoried through pharmacy and accounting.

Although far from being the solution to higher quality care, to increase speed and efficiency in hospitals, most centers are converting to Patient-Focused Care (PFC) which consists of:

1. Regrouping patients according to similar needs and services.
2. Cross-training caregivers to provide more of services patients need, increasing flexibility and improving continuity of care.
3. Managing quality and cost information at the PFC Center level.
4. Completing clinical pathways, increasing consistency and efficiency of care.
5. Physical moves within the hospital, flattening management structure, and speeding decision-making.
6. Appointing PFC Center co-directors, often non-physicians.

Aetna's CEO Ronald E. Comptom says: "Be quick, or be dead." Aetna salespersons print point-of-sale identification cards. Claims scanned into network computers supply instant claims service. Federal Express courier's carry tiny printers on belts that print instant labels. Only 20% of guests use hotel video check-out because it doesn't save *enough* time, and so hotels are trying room-faxed bills, and check-out machines. Airport and hotel van check-ins are trying bar-coded hand-held computers to speed up the process. In real estate, loan approval time is down from eight weeks to less than three days, home equity approvals are down from four hours to thirty minutes, and appraisals are submitted electronically the same day.

Ford has punched the fast-forward button as well: all the decision makers are brought together at critical times so months aren't wasted on the back-and-forth approval process. Long term assignments at Ford are five days.

> *Customers who have been spoiled*
> *by your competitors, won't wait for you.*

As Larry Wilson has stated in *Changing the Game* (1987), it's time to 'navigate, pay attention and take advantage.' That means moving fast and soon, and questioning all policies that slow you down. If you cannot compete on any other quality, you can make decisions, respond to customers, and come out with new products *faster* than your competitors.

Be first in the market before your competition comes in, driving down prices and profits. As Martin Sunde, regional general manager for IBM Southern California has said: "I'm trying to make this place run like a hospital emergency room, dropping one thing and running quickly to the next. Adaptability and speed is the name of the game."

A friend of mine was 62 days into the mortgage application approval process when the bank required extensive financial documentation that involved several thousand dollars' worth of accounting fees. The purchase had to be postponed because of the bank's inability to issue the mortgage within the escrow period prescribed in the purchase contract. Do you think these companies can compete with the new breed of lender? A TV commercial by Direct Trust, in Toronto, begins with a customer's phone call:

Customer:	"Hello, is this Direct Pizza?"
Company:	"No, this is Direct Trust."
Customer:	"Well, what do you sell?"
Company:	"We sell home loans, personal loans, and other financial services."
Customer:	"How long would it take you to get me a home mortgage? "
Company:	"Oh, about fifteen minutes"
Customer:	"I can't even get a pizza that quickly!"
Tag line:	*"If you would like to try this home loan by phone service call (###) ###-SAVE."*

People are not going to stand in line for forty-five days for a standard mortgage if someone will give them a customized, hassle-free home loan in a matter of minutes.

Speed spreads through all industries. Progressive Insurance uses an office van that includes a PC with modem, printer, fax, and two cellular phones, together with soft chairs and refreshments. The van can appear on the scene of an accident within fifteen minutes and settle the claim, including payment, within an hour and a half maximum. When physical injury is not involved, the insured is invited into the van, offered a soft drink while the report is filed and verified, and a check is issued on the spot. This cuts down on office expenses, tow charges, and storage, eliminates additional expenses incurred by lawyer involvement, and increases customer satisfaction.

How Companies Move Faster

1. Manufacture at the Point of Delivery.

Move the final production stages as close to the customer as possible. Printing and film processing have already moved production into the retail outlet. The traditional factory is disappearing in many businesses, and manufacture is moving down into the distribution and delivery systems. PC Connection moved their warehouses next to Airborne Express. Eyeglass lenses used to be made, stocked, and ground in a central location, and delivery took weeks. Lenscrafter moved the factory to the retail outlet so that glasses are ready in an hour. It's possible to get even closer.

2. Organize for speed.

The new company also helps its customers move faster. Xerox did a work flow analysis for Blue Cross/Blue Shield North Carolina and designed a customized publishing network that cut down the time it took to produce benefits booklet from 45 days to five days. Compaq ProLiant comes with an optional four-hour response time. Since Baltimore Gas and Electric (BGE) started instant response calls last year, many other utilities are following suit. BGE's Customer Information System dispatches within moments of a call, instead of the usual next day service. With personal communicators such as Personal Digital Assistants and modemed laptops, sales reps have instant product information access. Marriott's XPress Check-In eliminates the front desk computer and gives you a pre-cut key, reducing time from three to one-and-a-half minutes. Does that fraction count? Yes.

Customers must have direct and instant access, without call routing. FHP's President's Hotline handles direct calls. The Prudential Insurance Company has separate phone lines to handle different areas such as mental health, with all customer records on computer so that information is instantly available.

Customer expectations are based on time. Dan Burrus relays his experience with Marriott coffee service. The first time that a knock on the door occurred exactly at the time he requested coffee, Dan reckoned that it was a fluke. However, when it occurred consistently over several hotels, he investigated and found the reason. A computer-controlled kitchen times every activity, including the departure of the cart from the kitchen timed to arrive exactly at the time promised. Dan says because the bar has been raised by Marriott, every stay at a competitor becomes a potential disappointment.

Growing numbers of working women, overworked executives, and moonlighters are among the people who are increasingly willing to pay more money for things that save them time. Companies that handle household chores such as gardening, auto maintenance, and housecleaning are proliferating. Food companies have lost billions of dollars to fast-food chains over the years, and are trying to recapture these dollars by providing supermarkets with prepared meals and internet-based shops.

*The ability to deliver goods and services when
and where the customer chooses, is crucial to
success in the new marketplace.*

Link time-based competition to your customers and employees with a powerful information and service system; a feedback loop of customer knowledge. When the customers' three-year warranty is in its third year, Daiichi, a Tokyo-based appliance store, calls the customer and offers to send a trained technician to check the item for problems before the warranty expires. After the check, and before leaving, the technician offers to check any other appliances in the home as a courtesy, whether they were purchased from Daiichi or not. Customers fill out a detailed report on types, models and ages, and this is entered into on-line database available to the sales force. The home visit is followed with a letter, confirming the health of each item. In a short time, a salesperson calls with an invitation to their showroom to see a new oven replacing the one that's aging in the customer's home. About 70% of Daiichi sales are repeat customers, compared with 20% to other competitors.

3. Track *Your* Future, Not Your Competitor's.

Don't focus on the obvious enemy. If you are focused on the scorecard, you will miss the ball. If you are focused on beating others, you will miss opportunities to move fast to get new business. Competitors outside your industry are circling for the kill. The most serious threat to your survival may be your tendencies to throw snowballs at each other when someone else is out there with an UZI, planning to take you all out. Banks, keeping their eyes on their deposit and loan business, missed the wake up call to mutual funds until they watched Merrill Lynch and Fidelity walking out the back door with all their customers. Banks and financial service would be well served to cooperate.

Don't copy competitors—start with a blank slate. For example, to catch up with Campbell's Three-Minute Soup, the Lipton R&D team spent months trying to develop a competing Three-Minute Soup. Only when the team finally threw out the Campbell's Three-Minute mold, did they come up with an instant soup, and quickly gathered market share.

If you're spending valuable time tracking your competitors' movements, you're not only running in circles, but you're probably paying too much attention to the wrong target. It's the folks that you can't track—the ones that don't exist yet either as competitors, or even as companies—who are your real problems. That's because they're not worrying about tracking you. They're moving ahead with new offerings, redefining and reinventing the marketplace as they go along.

> *Don't imitate your competitors. Join them.*
> *Change the rules of the whole game.*

The cold war between archrivals Microsoft and Apple computer got colder with CEO Michael Spindler at the helm. However, with CEO Gilbert Amelio, competitors are becoming cooperators, and by the time this book is published, if Apple has not been acquired, Microsoft and Apple will most probably be considering a merger of at least some of their functions. Similarly, Oracle Corporation and Novell, Inc. share databases and products. Competitors are finally embedding in each others products, recognizing the ultimate good for their own survival as well as the benefit of the consumer.

Competing hospitals in five eastern and mid-west states now can obtain anti-trust protection when they work cooperatively to help reduce empty beds and under-used services. Cost-conscious hospitals share services from expensive technology to laundry. At the Southern California Healthcare System, dietary, lab services, housekeeping and laundry services have been, or will be, outsourced or shared. Six Canadian metal stamping companies and four steel makers teamed up for research, saving them all considerable development funds.

Be Flexible

Agility is the ability to make rapid change—to break out of a mass production model—and produce highly customized product when and where the customer wants, with economies of scope, not scale, and ever smaller niches. Agility is a major trait needed to thrive in a time of uncertain and unpredictable change. Be able to reconfigure systems, software, equipment, and organizational structure quickly. Build in agility to all contracts. However, to create agility, don't get too lean, because you'll be too fragile to withstand the impact of change. The downsized, lean organization can only do what it's doing, and nothing new. Honda Accord was so lean it couldn't respond fast enough, and lost out with a limited line. Although still struggling financially, Saturn allows changes in customer specifications up to four days prior to production. Over the years, Jostens Inc. has moved from high school rings and graduation photos, to educational software to multimedia educational systems to interactive cable TV for kids' homework.

If you're losing, be flexible enough to change the rules so that you're playing a game you can win. One debt-ridden hospital turned it's top floor into a hotel for visiting guests and is turning a profit and running 95% occupancy. Travel around your company and ask: "for what else and when else can this be used?" and "Why are we doing this?"

> *We have a coyote as a mascot—he can see both sides,*
> *he works fast alone or in pairs, plays dead to trick birds*
> *into coming close, and is never defeated by death.*
> CEO of a California hospital

After a decade of hit-or-miss efforts to speed product development and restructure, rigid Siemens has finally become more flexible. Gone are endless meetings, aimless research, and fear of taking risks. A new generation of managers is fostering cooperation across the company, and setting up teams to develop products and attack new markets. Since taking over in 1992, Siemens CEO Heinrich von Pierer has opened up Siemens for a financial airing. In 1994, he began disclosing profits and making managers answerable for the bottom line.

However, after he won the support of senior managers, he hit a brick wall. He was unable to turn thousands of bureaucrats into entrepreneurs. He started TOP—time-optimized processes, to encourage creativity, speed, and a market-focus. Von Pierer replaced their hierarchical structure and engineering

A two-volume report from the Agile Manufacturing Enterprise Forum (AMEF; Iacocca Institute, Lehigh University, 215/758-6351) called *21st Century Manufacturing Enterprise Strategy*, describes how manufacturing concerns will evolve in the next 15 years. The AMEF menu includes: greater product customization, advanced networking, quick introduction, upgradable products, emphasis on trained, knowledgeable workers, interactive customer relationships, and reconfiguration of production process.

focus with a new emphasis on innovation and service, set up special teams to develop products and markets faster, and appointed new-thought managers. Change *is* possible.

Fail Forward Faster. Flexibility means being able to drop what doesn't work. How long does it take for you, or your company, to recognize failure? Sometimes we drag failure out for months, years, even decades. Refusing to accept failure consumes time and resources that could be invested in the next success. United States consumer electronics, steel, textile, and auto manufacturers took more than a decade to fail before they seriously began to change their processes.

Use the 6-6 Rule. Question everything you have been doing for over six months; if you have been doing it for that long, it may be losing money, or may be excess baggage.

You may be obsolete in 18 months not because someone else will obsolete you, but because you will obsolete yourself. If you are doing things the same way you did them last year, you may be your own worst competitor. Be ready to switch immediately and let go of what you had.

The outfitting company Pategonia created their clothes with an exclusive propylene, but others made copies and sold them for less. Pategonia no longer had the exclusive, nor were they price leaders. In short order, they switched to capalene, and consumers could again identify a difference. The patent owner of a bicycle seat called a 'Terry,' discovered other seats on the market remarkably similar to hers that were selling for significantly less. The owner figured that by the time the copyright attorneys had finished, she would have been bankrupt. So she created a new design and got it into the market fast. If you don't compete, you obsolete yourself and others. Most of your competition is with yourself, and the current ways you do business.

Make sensible policy change a way of life. Update your own

personal blueprints at the same time: how many old rules are you keeping that served you in the past? When elephants calves were tied to chain with a small bell, as adults they couldn't move when the chain was reattached, even if it isn't anchored. Habits stick like plaque unless they're removed regularly. Are you stuck with policies that don't make sense?

If you find that you are advising your employees that they can't make changes because of rules, try what we mentioned that a California Credit Union had tried. Because they recognized that true progress would be made only when they were freed of their own bureaucratic build-up, Hughes Federal Credit Union held a Dumb Rules Contest among their employees. They received over 400 suggestions of dumb rules that they were following that either impeded their work, created costs or decreased revenue. They reviewed all of them and found that even though they could drop less than half of the dumb rules, they still saved a large sum of money. For those rules that they could not change because of regulations of which the staff were not aware, the exercise became an opportunity to clear up misperceptions.

One plastics company gave awards for the person or department that demonstrated that they had been able to break with an outdated restrictive rule. It had to be in line with the company's new vision and demonstrate how it saved time or money. They called it the Cow-Tipper Award; every Friday they assembled, wrote down the outdated regulation or rule ('sacred cow') on the side of a cardboard cut-out of a cow. Then the employee or department were recognized, given a Cow Tipper Pin, and either cash or a day off work was awarded. Others have developed similar rule-cutting ceremonies. To demonstrate the important of 'cutting through the red tape,' one company gives away large spray-painted gold scissors in a weekly ceremony. One caution, however: these awards and ceremonies are meant to reflect a deeper change into which all staff buy in. They will be resented if they are substitutes for fundamental change.

One of Johnson & Johnson's bases for success lies in their ability to let go of failing units before they become leaden monkeys. The inability to let go when needed is one of the top five psychological predictors of business failure (Richter, 1996). Learn to let go.

> *Business fails because of what they won't give up.*
> Peter Drucker

Develop Small Business Units
Smaller businesses who are highly focused serving community or market niches can thrive in tomorrow's marketplace. Unfortunately, smaller business too often concentrates on the competition, or the larger players, and miss the very opportunities and advantages they have due to their small and nimble size.

> *The bigger the global economy,*
> *the more important the smaller parts.*
> John Naisbitt

In the digital revolution, basement-run businesses can and do compete on level playing fields with internationals, according to Taylor & Archer (1994) in *Up against the Wal-Marts: How your Business can Prosper in the Shadow of the Retail Giants*. A key example—comparatively small Southwest Airlines, is leading with 31% market share, higher than American and United combined. The giants scrambled to remold after Southwest with mixed results. Southwest CEO Herb Kelleher is not only the founder, but also the head cheerleader of this thriving airline. Dressed as the Easter Bunny or Elvis, he boards the aircraft and chats with crew and passengers. He's tried profit-sharing schemes, buddy systems, and open contests, and they all work. His airline attracts over 100 applications for every position. Southwest, like General Electric, Emerson Electric, Johnson and Johnson, AT&T in their 1995 split, and Motorola have kept, or have been forced to keep, their sights focused on small. Johnson &

Johnson is a collection of 168 small companies selling everything from Band-Aids to baby powder.

Think and act small, we'll be bigger.
Think and act big, and we'll be smaller.
Herb Kelleher

It's easier for small organizations to act like big ones these days. Scale and sophistication are no longer the prerogatives of the Fortune 500. Today, small organizations do what big ones can do, including operating on a global basis, attracting consumers, building virtual linkages to other partners, and participating fully in the value chain.

How Small Companies Focus:

1. Get Market-Savvy. They know the demographics of their customer base and shop their competitors, price-compete on staples and consumer-tracked items, then offer splurge items that can't be comparison-shopped.

2. Join Up. They form a buying cooperative. Towson Computers in Baltimore teamed up with five other independents to form an alliance with a MicroAge franchiser for a double-win alliance: they purchase from MicroAge at a lower cost and MicroAge profits from increased business.

3. Fill in the Blanks. Fiore's competes with Blockbuster Video in Memphis with lesser known and classic videos. Colorado Trinidad Builders Supply has items not at Wal-Mart. In addition to, or instead of, stock carried by the superstore, find a narrow, deep niche. For example, be the only shoe store in the country with all possible variations of high-end running shoes, and hire staff who can become industry experts.

4. Can't Beat 'Em, Join' Em. Small Towson Computers helps superstore CompUSA with tough diagnoses and repairs: a win-win. Small Minneapolis-based Baxter's Books and NYC Verso Books go toe-to-toe with Barnes & Noble by offering hard-to-find titles.

5. Provide the absolutely greatest shopping experience *ever.* Create unpaid sales advocates for yourself; people who will sell you free because you're fabulous. Give your customers not just 'smiles in the aisles' but 'memorable experiences.' Hire people who know how to kid-glove and sweet-talk customers. Baum's women clothes hangs bathrobes in the changing room. A grocery store entertains and hands out small toys to kids.

6. Be fast. Florida-based Renaissance Cars Inc. won against the big three with the high-performance low-cost electric car Tropica. They were first. Procter and Gamble sped up their development-release cycle such that products are now rolled out in four months. Chrysler cut product development time from four-and-a-half years to three years by using a platform team working together.

7. Compete Up and Down the Market and the Scale
Many of the companies with whom I consult are scrambling to match price competition, and recognize the competitive scale. Don't be tempted to drop prices too quickly. For example, if two competing GEM stores offer an item at $1.00, and one store decides to get business by price, the item goes to 95c, both drop, and who wins? Price competition is a fool's game, or, the death of a thousand cuts.

Summary
Focus on actions, not promise. Rework the institution so that actions promote, rather than discourage, learning. Without changes in the way that work gets done and that mistakes get treated, so that only the potential for improvements exists.

Reorganize for speed. Compete with yourself and be ready to drop whatever no longer works. The small company can win.

1. Stop knowing and start asking. Who are your customers and non-customers? What's important to them?

2. List what your competitors do that you don't.

3. Identify what works and build on it.

4. If you want increased revenue, reduced costs, and process time to improve, hit these areas directly rather than through the back door with indirect quality programs.

 Look back over the notes you've made in the margins in this chapter. Condense them into two action points; two changes you will make as a result of reading this section.

Actions I will take:

1._____

2._____

Chapter Six
Building a Better Path

*Leaders of the industrial economy built railroad
tracks and highways. Leaders in the information age
build empires on electronic tracks that direct
the movement of an industry's information.
Don't build a better mousetrap, build a better path.*

That's where the money is.
Bank robber Willie Sutton, when asked why he robbed banks

New Channels. Better paths. More paths. Where are *your* customers? Set up shop near them. Shoppers are overwhelmed with new products and services vying for their disposable income. Each year, more than 4,000 new supermarket and drugstore products flood the market. Many consumers may never see many of the new products because manufacturers fail to recognize that the only competitive advantage is to build a better path.

Hundreds of new distribution channels and outlets are springing up every month, from discount stores and warehouses to upscale boutiques and home delivery, and from specialty dealers to hypermarkets. Consumers have generally not only responded well to the alternatives, they have come to expect and demand the diversity. Catalogs, toll-free numbers, discounters, and one-stop convenience centers all have become part of the marketing vernacular. And all have become part of the consumer's expectations.

Change *where* you sell. Customers shop everywhere. Even MTV is starting a shopping service. Bell Atlantic offers InfoTravel. City Key Interactive Video from US West Marketing Resources sells to hotel guests 24-hours a day. On-Command Video is now in 10,000 rooms with print and transaction capacity. The Las Vegas Hospitality Network shows instructional gaming, retails, gives cash advances, sells show tickets and prints coupons. Guest use is automatically tracked. Promus Hotels, representing Embassy Suites, Hampton Inn and Homewood Suites, are one of many on the World Wide Web, where prospective guests can preview properties, layouts, and local interest.

The Greater Southeast Health Care System set up blood pressure screenings in Praise the Lord Barber shops in Washington, D.C. Bankers now sell more Certificates of Deposit in supermarkets than in banks, and bank branches in supermarkets are growing at twenty percent pre year. McDonalds Corporation have entered hospitals, and now provide food service for over twenty centers.Chicago's O'Hare and Minneapolis airports have full medical facilities. Riverside Methodist in Columbus, Ohio, has opened a health clinic at a local food pantry, and Orlando Regional Medical Center has door-to-door immunizations. American Greetings 'Creatacard' kiosks are in office buildings; Food franchises such as Subway, McDonalds, and Burger King are at your Texaco service station. Texas has a fleet of 50 ATM-like government information kiosks, to be installed in malls, grocery stores and other high-traffic areas, to give out information on government jobs, retraining, and will soon conduct DMV transactions.

Make Contact Easier. An 800 number for service is only the beginning; make it easy for your customers to get to you. MicroLam Products not only has an 800 number for service, but also the home phone number of every general manager. The perception is that management *is available.*

During the coming decade, contact will not only be easier but will be just-in-time direct to manufacturers with a central information center located anywhere with an 800 or 900 number (or more likely, on the internet), which will direct orders to distribution and delivery channels where the final manufacture will take place.

Tighten or Shrivel Distribution Channels

The mid-size squeeze out continues, with the very large and the very small specialized or super-service stores the survivors. The mid-level distribution squeeze is just beginning. Distributors are being dropped from the chain unless there is a no more cost-effective way of reaching the end consumer. With grocery margins around one or two percent, distribution centers are disappearing and automated racking systems are blossoming. Sophisticated information systems handle everything from studying consumer buying patterns to targeting ads. Technology is bridging the manufacturer-consumer gap in every industry.

For example, Fidelity Investments uses the Web to distribute information, and to locate new customers. As manufacturers rethink their distribution channels, FedEx, UPS and other carriers will be crucial to their success as customers expect and get same-day sample delivery. Technology and distribution shifts challenge not only banks: travel agents, stockbrokers, and real estate and insurance agents all feel the squeeze. Over thirty-three percent of banks sell insurance in 34 states, such that with direct marketing, sales through stockbrockers, toll-free and internet sales, insurance agents now write only thirty two percent of the personal market. Toll-free and mass market sales have grown to seven percent of the personal insurance market. With commissions down, surviving agents and brokers will choose to control both distribution and technology or become, as Robert Hunter of Consumer Federation of America has termed: "the buggy-whip makers of today's economy."

Customers are using Ameritech and Citibank screen phones for banking services, browsing through classified ads and picking up theatre tickets. The phones, with credit card swipes for instant purchases, are one step closer to TV banking. The Bank Administration Institute says 57% of banking transactions are already outside branches. Mergers and acquisitions closed 2,454 bank branches last year; and one of five branches will close at end of decade, as consumers turn to ATM's and electronic delivery. Although ATM's may not close banks, they have replaced tellers. In some regions, demand is up for the Canadian style a-bank-on-every-corner, with mini-branches set up in malls and new subdivisions. However, banks look more like retail stores and supermarkets. State and federal laws make it clumsy for banks to underwrite insurance, but they can sell it, and sell it they do. Signet Banking, offering a 6.9% credit card rate, already markets personal, auto and homeowners insurance. The customer is the focus and the best path captures his attention.

Insurance companies are negotiating with banks and competing with their own agents. Travelers Insurance Company and Metropolitan Life Insurance are developing new distribution channels. Mergers and consolidations such as Metropolitan Life Insurance and New England Mutual are becoming more and more commonplace. Direct-response firms such as Allstate Corporation and State Farm Mutual Automobile Insurance Company cut costs to between twelve and sixteen percent, with new direct response companies down to ten percent.

To thrive, master the new technology,
become indispensable to your customers, narrow your
suppliers, and find a focused niche market.

Not only airlines are cutting travel agents from their network, relocation companies reach customers directly. PHH Homequity's MovePlus lets individuals access services previously reserved for corporations. Apple and IBM market to the end user. Manufacturers are providing direct electronic query, decision support, order entry, and near-immediate delivery to the customer. Customers can scan options and enter orders directly twenty-four hours a day. Federal Express customers enter parcel pickup requests directly into its master route schedule through a touch-tone telephone. Citicorp's Citiline service, like all other major banks, let customers access their account balances, make loans, verify checks and deposits, and transfer funds without human assistance.

Real estate's once closely-guarded Multiple Listing Service is easily accessed by customers. Although sales are now still limited on the internet, there are virtual reality systems that lead customers through rooms and around properties, complete with sound and smells. Although the technology is not widely available and still expensive, wise brokers don't ignore the go-direct implications. To avoid the six percent that agents now earn, the largest opportunity in real estate might be in the electronic brokerage business. While we await our future virtual world, any broker activity could be complemented by an information service that brings buyers and sellers together. Presently, buyers use terminals to search through video clips of properties that meet their size, price, and location criteria and then contact the listing broker or the seller directly.

Coldwell Banker Corporation offers real estate shoppers pictures of homes, neighborhoods and traffic patterns from satellite. Within five years, we will be able to get live, high resolution photographs of far-off places ten times clearer than best residential private system. Television stations started offering related services over ten years ago, with half-hour shows picturing houses for sale. With complex interactive TV screens, properties may begin to sell without physical tours, and perhaps even without brokers, especially to foreign investors. It could even lead to remote purchases of real estate properties, particularly in countries with disadvantaged trade and currency positions. An acquaintance told me that one day he was sitting on his dock in Northern Ontario, leisurely 'surfing' the net on his laptop for real estate listings in Vancouver. He discovered what appeared to be the home of his dreams, called the agent on his cell phone, who picked up the call on *his* cell phone. My acquaintance flew to Vancouver the next day, made an offer on the property the same day, and a day later the deal was closed. Business anywhere, anytime, goes to whomever will build the better path.

Citicorp has competed successfully against the giant German Deutsche Bank on its own soil. Citicorp is growing at twenty-six percent per year in Germany just doing what it does best, combining technology with North American service. Deutsche Bank wasn't paying attention when in came 24-hour teller machines, telephone banking, and a clear youth market focus. Focus on what you do best and flaunt it world-wide.

Superior Livestock Auction uses satellite transmission, television cameras, and computerized buying networks to auction steers. It saves the time and cost of trucking, and eliminates the risk of injury and disease. More than a million cattle were sold over this network in 1990. Electronic used car auctions are transmitted to wholesalers who place bids electronically. A major grain elevator and brokerage company, Data Transmission Network, sends spot grain prices, futures quotes, and weather and other farm information to over 50,000 customers, and has a stock market valuation in excess of $100 million.

By 2005, virtually everyone will be connected and tens of thousands of specialty markets will appear. For example, Videotex provides electronic malls for entrepreneurs to set up shop alongside giant retail chains. Those who do well will offer convenience, lower cost, more choice, faster response, ease of use, more processing capability, mass customizing, and previewing of future outcomes. American Greetings' Creatacards has spread globally, and contains neighborhood-specific language computer-discs, including French-Canadian. The kiosks are common in retail and shopping outlets, office lobbies, airports, and other high-traffic areas. American also has super-tight inventory and cost-control, fast production times, and are masters at teaming,' for example, with Ralston-Purina with cards for pet-lovers.

Store information centrally and make it available to customers over a network. Put your information inside telephones, televisions, computers, cars, and other products. Otis Elevator Company created Otis-Line Service so that if anything goes wrong in one of its boxes, it is diagnosed and, if possible, self-corrected within the box. Otherwise, a message is sent to the servicing office about what parts, labor, and maintenance are needed. The real profit is in the service contract.

Encyclopedia Britannica's electronic home encyclopedia is stored on optical storage discs accessed by entering requests onto a special home terminal or appropriate PC. Digital Equipment Corporation's (DEC) entire software library can be put on one CD-ROM and installed together with a CD-ROM reader inside every box they sell. DEC embeds all of its software in a physical product on the customers' premises. Then, it charges for usage by taking a remote meter reading. Customers have access to the full range of DEC software, but only pay for what they use. Put a meter and a modem into every 'box' you build. Whether it's a high-definition television or a desktop computer, or any appliance or electronic device, connect it with information services and install a built-in billing mechanism. The meter and modem are loss leaders. The real profits lie in the traffic, not in the boxes. Set-top boxes with giveaway interactive services, and phones delivered through cable, will grow by 65% a year to $31 billion by 2005.

On Microsoft Network's channel, Kodak's Kodalux customers can home-computer preview photos they have dropped off, decide which they want, and send them to relatives on-line. The *Wall Street Journal's Personal Journal* lets you select your favorite columns, companies and stocks. Your personal edition is then delivered to your computer each morning. Safeway's Pea Pod Grocery internet-based service will shop for you and deliver to your home.

> *The one who controls the communication port*
> *into the home will be in a great position.*
> Gregory Ehlers

Teco Energy's box controls power and data signals going through house wiring. A computer attaches to the meter with phone and cable inputs, can read the meter, relay signals to appliances, and will eliminate the descrambler. Mondex microchipped plastic cards for electronic funds transfer are testing in England and Canada; Visa tested their smart card at the 1996 Olympic Games. With a Boston Chicken and Comcast Metrophone's team-up, punch in a given number that connects you to the closest Boston Chicken, get directions, and pick up your food in a no-wait line. Walgreen's 24-hour online Intercom Plus touch-tone phone system takes prescription refill orders and transfers them directly to the pharmacy's computer. The system then measures and dispenses the prescription, resulting in an almost 100% increase in number filled, and no need for more staff. Toronto's Mount Sinai Hospital's PC-based bedside system digitizes voice records, outputs and distributes forms automatically, and will soon be at every bedside.

> *Link buyers and sellers, producers and consumers,*
> *upstream and downstream, providers and users,*
> *and senders and receivers.*

Fine-tune your focus to tight groups of consumers. Infomercials will be selected by computer to show only to targeted markets. People will be able to choose television without commercials. The specificity of each channel will mean that fewer will watch, but with a highly focused group. Only $1000 in advertising will yield 30,000 people who will buy your product. Color printers can turn out magazines from atop a television set. Time Warner will be able to zap a marketing brochure to a targeted television at a lower cost than the Postal Service. Create an easier path to the consumer but better, control the path.

Set up a consumer chat line similar to Saturn's so someone who are thinking of buying your product can ask people who have one, how they like it.

The better path to the customer in health care means developing a better path for the patient to travel toward caring for his or her own health. Building a better path, telemedicine will create a cost-effective and efficient health-care system, allowing health-care professionals to focus where they are needed the most: to supervise educational programming helping our population stay healthy, and treating serious disease.

Summary
Understand that the distribution squeeze affects everyone.
Go where your customers are.
Control communication into the home or business.
Embed intelligence into your product or service.

 Look back over the notes you've made in the margins in this chapter. Condense them into two action points; two changes you will make as a result of reading this section.

Actions to take:

1._____

2._____

Chapter Seven
The Company's Mind

Changing behavior alone is like wagging the dog's tail in an effort to make him happy. To affect permanent change, the beliefs upon which behavior rests need to be changed. Beliefs are the foundation of behaviors.

Vice President Al Gore's 1993 promise to reinvent government in the first year of the Clinton Administration, produced a nationwide yawn. The Republicans' 1995 'Contract With America,' initially met with no better a response. Press release after press release has announced the reinvention of yet another agency or program; big conferences have been convened, and television appearances made. Yet these efforts have met with little, or no, real change. Why?

Any organization, whether biological or social, must change its basic structure if it significantly changes its size. Similarly, any organization, business or a government agency, needs to rethink itself once it is more than forty or fifty years old. It has outgrown its policies and its rules of behavior. If it continues in its old ways, it usually becomes ungovernable, unmanageable, and uncontrollable. There is no point in blaming Presidents for the disarray of our government. It is the fault not of the Democrats nor the Republicans nor Liberals nor

Conservatives nor the New Democratic Party. Government has outgrown the structure. But the policies, and the rules designed for it, are still in use.

Why Do Organizations Fail to See the Future?

A company's, (or a country's!) founder developed a vision of a particular market and an organization to optimize that market, and this worked well at the time. As competition shifted, customers changed, new technologies appeared, the company had a choice. It could either develop systems to track external changes, or it could fail to make the most of new opportunities because it was still doing its best to make the most of old ones.

> *Those who fail to see the future are still doing*
> *their best to make the most of the past.*

Here's what happens. The original vision structured the perceptions and acts of employees. The company's processes, assumptions, rules, and behaviors became woven into all levels. Typically, because few structures controlled for changes in markets, top managers who finally try to catch up with an escaping market, are blocked by the inertial force of their original structure. These must be recognized before changes can be made.

When signs of trouble finally do get through to them, senior managers still try to avoid evidence that contradicts expectation. They glorify the past, and find ways to justify current practice. Managers seek answers to the wrong questions, hire consultants who gather worthless data, and they institute quick-fix programs. Rigid, blindfolding structures cause managers to ignore complaints that might provide valuable, life-saving information. 'Groupthink' (agreeing in public and disagreeing in private), 'blaming,' and 'communication paralysis' are three common defensive symptoms in dysfunctional companies.

Rethinking

The first reaction in a chaotic situation, is to do what current governments are doing–patching. Patching always fails. The next step is to downsize, where management picks up the axe and lays about itself indiscriminately. However, as pointed out in Chapter Two, these are rarely, if ever, viable long-term solutions.

Every agency, every policy, every program, every activity, should be confronted with these questions:

What is our mission?
Is it still the right mission?
Is it still worth doing?

If we were not already doing this,
would we now go into it?

By not asking these questions, many organizations have been off-track for years. For example, the Occupational Safety and Health Administration (OSHA) runs on the assumption that an unsafe environment is the primary cause of accidents, and so it tries to do the impossible: create a risk-free world. Although eliminating safety hazards is the right thing to do, it's only one part of safety, and probably the lesser part. In fact, by itself it achieves next to nothing. The most effective way to produce safety is to eliminate unsafe behavior. OSHA's definition of an accident, "when someone gets hurt," is inadequate. To cut down on accidents, the definition should be "a violation of the rules of safe behavior, whether anyone gets hurt or not." Only rethinking basic meanings will significantly change OSHA. Rethinking will result in a list, with activities and programs that should be strengthened at the top, ones that should be abolished at the bottom, and between them, activities that need to be refocused or in which a few hypotheses might be tested. Rethinking is not primarily concerned with cutting expenses. It is concerned with increases in performance, in quality, and in service. Cost savings can emerge as a by-product.

When a company is deeply examined, a set of beliefs about change and about the organization is typically revealed. These beliefs function as filters of information, and thus are rarely examined or questioned. They just are. They exert a strong influence over what actions will or will not be taken. To change, what's needed is to not only change functions and forms, but company beliefs. When the Bell system let go of old values, traditions, and ways of thinking in order to create new structures and systems, in the context of new visions, only then did they began to experience success.

There are four distinct set of beliefs that emerge based on the world view of the senior management or the original founder. Most beliefs were formed during the industrial age, and are inadequate to carry a company into the future. If unchanged, they will block change.

Stage 1: Fix-It Thinking
"If it ain't broke, don't fix it!" or "Don't mess with what's working," is more than resistance to change. It is the expression of a very deep belief system rooted in the past, in an earlier, mechanistic era.

As you will see in Chapter Fourteen, whatever is threatening to the system will be resisted. Those who are the 'fixers' will be threatened when things they have repaired, break. If the organization is a machine, it should run smoothly. Leaders should be engineers who calculate standards, maintain equipment, and set controls. When the machine breaks down, a mechanic 'fixes it.' Change means something has broken. External repair persons in the form of consultants or a new CEO are resisted, because they imply psychologically that folks have broken something.

A west-coast electric utility with which I consulted was faced with many problems: new independent power producers as

competitors, higher costs and overhead, and increased customer demands. Top executives, all engineers, were caught in
a machine view. The Chief Engineer ordered his senior people
to "fix things." They found nothing was broken, and nothing
changed. Next, they held retreats to discover what was broken. These problems were fixed and everyone thought that
things would go back to normal. Things got worse.
Employees went on strike. Managers blamed supervisors and
supervisors blamed employees. As things got worse, the Chief
Engineer called in more management consultants, some of
whom bought into their world view and started tinkering
with Total Quality Management programs to fix the company. The consultants who advised: "Re-think your whole business," insulted the Chief Engineer, who concluded that the
consultants really didn't understand how the business
worked.

Stage 2: Block-Building Thinking
Block-building thinking also builds on the past but leads to
better performance over time. One builds on a foundation to
achieve higher levels of performance. The organization is
described as if it were 'under construction.' Developmental
change agents are referred to as trainers, coaches, or developers and are asked to do organizational 'development' or team
'building' to 'improve' performance, 'increase' capabilities, or
build competencies.

For example, a nursing association held a series of strategy
sessions to build and develop the association. They focused
on 'building membership' and 'developing' new features.
They ignored the more radical changes they needed, which
was to merge with another group, because they were just
developing what they had always had.

Stage 3: Switched Thinking
Switched thinking involves a move from one state or condition to another, such as the move from handwritten to auto-

mated data entry, or from a centralized to a decentralized system. Terms such as 'relocating,' 'moving forward,' 'knowing the right path,' and 'taking the best route' are common. Change agents here are planners or guides because they are familiar with the journey and with what to expect along the way. For example, a large Canadian food processing plant introduced a new technology. Meetings were held with the union to insure that everyone was on board, that things stayed on track, and that the road ahead stayed clear. After following a detailed schedule and timetable, every one in the plant celebrated the arrival of the new equipment. No one ever considered working on other changes such as re-designing jobs or the reward system because "our job was to move to a new way of manufacturing, not create a whole new plant."

Stage 4: Jump-Shift Thinking
Jump-Shift thinking implies a break from one state of being to a different state of being, for example, from a regulated monopoly to a market-driven competitive business. The language used reflects an alteration in the state of being, as in becoming a different organization. Terms are used such as 'awakening,' 'uncovering,' 'escaping,' 'purifying,' 'enlightening,' 'returning to the core,' 'unfolding,' 'dying and being reborn.' Change agents are asked to help folks to 'wake up,' 'remove the blinders,' 'get out of the box,' 'get rid of excess baggage,' 'see the light,' and 'recreate ourselves.' The change agent is referred to as a 'liberator,' 'visionary,' or 'creator' who can help see the new possibilities of the new organization.

Assess your Belief System
Assess your company's belief system by content-analyzing a selection of memos. Pay attention to how someone speaks or writes about change. Know which belief(s) people and groups of people are using, and whether or not they are aware of it. Bring these images to people's attention. Then begin to use

appropriate change images. Don't confuse people by using inappropriate or incongruent images.

> *Images are powerful. The belief or beliefs one uses to help define what is happening will lead to differing courses of action.*

 Our actions naturally tend to follow our assessments. When you have assessed the images you use, continue to check all communications.

1. Listen to the word images you and others use to describe the change effort for clarity, consistency, and comprehension.

2. Work to align the language system to help get people working in unison.

3. Shape how people think about the change through the creative use of images and symbols.

> *Pay attention to how you and others describe change, both verbally and in writing. Make sure what you say is what you mean. Don't talk about building on the past if what you really want to do is escape the past and create a new future.*

Treat Change Viruses

When I visit organizations in which externals of change are in place, but nothing is improving, in addition to language problems, I often find one of several 'corporate viruses.' If ignored, they can fatally infect the whole organization. These are three of the most common:

1. Undergrounditis. The subjective, subtle, underground and unwritten rules clash with the written. 'Who to get close to, who to avoid, who to blame, and who to fear' paralyze behavior. People who 'can't play the game' are shunted aside. Treatment: Base decisions on objective and open criteria. Talk openly in groups about unwritten rules.

2. Kitchen-sinkitis. All desirable goals are equally prioritized: customers, productivity, safety, and quality. Although these are all key—with a wide focus, you shoot nothing. What's worse, employees are so confused, they do nothing. To disinfect, decide on one clear priority at a time. Review everything you send out for clarity and consistency. Ask select groups once a quarter about what they perceive as important, what they think are the company goals, and what are their priorities. Then correct what has gone off-track.

3. Changitis. Inspired by Tom Peters, one City Manager believed that he was cutting edge by communicating chaos, but his managers were dispirited and burning out. People do not thrive on chaos. People can tolerate unlimited change over which they perceive control, but constant, uncontrolled, last-minute program-du-jour change is debilitating. Treatment: Make sure changes are focused on specific end results or a clear vision, planned carefully, and talked about openly. People resist meaningless, irrelevant change unrelated to their jobs and to the company's direction, but welcome change that makes sense.

Signs of Company-Wide Resistance

1. Blaming. When these symptoms are present, there are clear victims and victimizers, much blame and fault finding, collusion and triangling, and much time wasted managing conflict and disorganization. People are busy finding out who did it instead of solving the problem. They spend time plotting revenge, resenting others, and sabotaging others' efforts.

2. Buffering. Buffering means creating a buffer between the work of an organization and actual productivity. The goal is to express anger toward the company. The strength of the thought disorder is greater than the push for success. Sabotaging, canceling at the last minute, giving insufficient resources for projects, verbal support with no follow through, the formation of more committees, and the ignoring of reports are common symptoms of buffering.

3. Triangling. "It's us against them. Let me tell you how terrible it is, and awful he is." Triangles form when Employee A has a difficulty with Employee B, but because of fear or lack of skills, instead of solving the problem with person B, Employee A allies, or triangles with, Employee C. Employee C completes the triangle when he or she commiserates or allies with Employee B against Employee A. If unchecked, triangles can spread quickly through an organization, destroying energy and weakening strengths.

4. Group Think. The Abilene Paradox described by Harvey (1988) is a set of conditions in which people join in group-think situations to perpetuate a thought disorder: People know the problem, they know what to do about it, they keep information from those in charge, they all decide to do things that waste time and aren't productive, and they continue being frustrated and dissatisfied.

What To Do
1. Expose the Belief. If you expose the belief, you do change it a bit, but at the risk of being ostracized or fired. For example, a teenager diagnosed as a schizophrenic often comes from a 'schizophrenic family,' meaning the whole family has a serious thought disorder. The theory held by many family theorists is that the teenager, by expressing symptoms, is challenging the dysfunction of the family. Thus, the teenager who is diagnosed may be the healthiest part of the system.

*Problems seldom exist at the level
at which they're expressed.*

However, the severity of the family disorder is such that the challenge must be ignored if the family is to remain intact and in denial. Thus, the teenager is ostracized by the family and labeled 'sick.' If you work in a dysfunctional organization, which many are, first gather a critical mass of persons behind and beside you if you want to confront an unhealthy system.

Anyone has the power to change a system.

2. Listen and acknowledge. Encourage people to express themselves clearly, and offer good conflict management skill training.

Get support to sell solutions. What's important to people in charge? Stop colluding. Request triangle break up. Focus on the problem, not the person.

Summary
Unexamined rules and beliefs can prevent change.
Analyze the type of thinking used by individuals, or company-wide, by appearance of key words.
There are viruses that can infect the whole organization if left unchecked.
Exposure of beliefs is often enough to help create change.

 Look back over the notes you've made in the margins in this chapter. Condense them into two action points; two changes you will make as a result of reading this section.

Actions to take:

1._____

2._____

Chapter Eight
Positioning Yourself

If your model for 'normal' is the 1960's, '70s or '80s, you will never get back to normal. 'Normal' is based on a whole set of global economic conditions that no longer apply.

As novelist Thomas Wolfe stated in one of his book titles, *You Can't Go Home Again because Home isn't There Anymore.*

Are you a distributor or intermediary of information or services, such as a real estate agent/broker, insurance agent/broker, or travel agent? Suppliers are giving customers direct, on-line access to their computerized ordering and inventory systems.

Are you in the speaking or training business? Company-owned and industry-wide TV networks and internet communication will gather more and more of meetings budgets.

Are you in the publishing business? In 1994, CD-ROM hit a flash point, when the information on electronic media exceeded the information on paper. Although newspaper circulation growth grew from thirty-eight million in 1975 to eighty million in 1995, the 6.8 million people who read online will blossom as paper goes digital.

Are you in hospital-based health care? Over 50 percent of hospitals are predicted to close within five years, and up to 76% of physician specialists will be surplus in a capitated environment.

Has it been more than ten years since you completed a college degree in your field or specialty? Up to 80% of what you know may be wrong. Eighty-five percent of the information in National Institutes of Health computers is upgraded every five years. Our compiled knowledge doubles every year. An advanced degree in any area will hold for only about six to eight years. In higher technology areas, knowledge is being replaced every two to three years. Given these rapid refresh rates, it's not a matter of *whether* you will need to change your knowledge set, but *how often.*

The traditional career path has dead ended. By 2001, only one person in every 50 will be promoted, compared to 1:20 in 1987. By 2000, eighty-five percent of the United States labor force will be working for firms employing fewer than 200 people. Only thirty-nine percent of employed persons state that they intend to be in the same job in five years. People change careers, on the average, every ten years. Thus, given a life expectancy of roughly eighty years, we might have up to six careers during a lifetime. The good news is that up to six million jobs will open for professionals, executives, and technicians in high-skill service occupations. Those who are hired will be future-skilled: techno-literate, flexible, and people-skill oriented. The only bad news is if you haven't developed these skills.

The question is not, "do I need to change?"
It is, "what do I need to do and how quickly
do I need to do it?"

We don't want people to come to us as a marriage.
We want them to think of it as dating.
Don't come here for security; come here for excitement.

The contract between employer and employee may have changed forever. Ray Smith, CEO of Bell Atlantic, has said, "Once in the corporation, the employee's own skills, talent, and personality must bring them to the fore, because the corporation isn't really tracking people." Bell Atlantic's training courses are now stored in the computers, and employees are responsible for learning what's available and mastering the content. Job openings are listed in the computer, and employees are responsible for knowing what's available and applying for the position. Most importantly, at Bell Atlantic, employees are responsible for increasing their value to the company. There's nothing in Smith's message about taking care of employees. Being taken care of will not be part of the new corporate commitment.

As it becomes employee's responsibility to keep their skills up and to be visible making a difference, they will accept more responsibility for themselves and make new assessments of their value to the organization, of whether or not they fit in, and if they are accepted and respected.

Create initiatives in which you can demonstrate you value. Make sure you have breadth, and at least one area in depth. Position yourself so you're a key player in the loop. Become a person whose views are respected. Be selective in accepting assignments that give you an opportunity to shine as individuals. Do work that lets you say, 'In 1996, I was responsible for gaining x number of customers, saving y number of dollars, increasing revenues by z.'

As security and paternalism end, become more selfish about where you work and what you do. Become proactive and strategic about your career, the jobs you accept, and the assignments you take. To a far greater extent than before,

What Good are You?*

Increase your corporate survival by assessing and communicating your value to your employer. Think of yourself as the president of your own business, contracting services to your present employer. You should be able to answer these questions:

1. WHAT DO YOU DO?
What is the product or service you produce? How good is it, compared to the competition? What should be done to improve it?

2. WHAT IS EXPECTED OF YOU?
What goals does your employer have for you? How do your skills qualify you to do this?

3. CAN YOU PROVE YOUR WORTH?
How do you measure your results? How do you measure your staff's results?

4.CAN YOU GROW WITH THE COMPANY?
How do you improve your firm's bottom line? How can you change your job so it will cost less to support and produce more revenue? What new skills should you develop? Where else in the company can your skills be used?

5. CAN YOU COMMUNICATE WHAT YOU DO?
Can you explain all this so that your eight-year-old understands? Make sure your successes get communicated to all levels. Keep your message simple, clear and compelling.

* in your employer's eyes?

guide your decisions by whether or not the outcome will be good for *you*. This means that an increase in employee self-interest is necessary at the same time that organizations need a commitment to optimizing the good of the whole. This conflict is modulated by the reality that the individual's self-interests are best served if the organization is successful.

> *Work is a meritocracy. In a meritocracy, commitment is conditional on performance, and performance is always competitive. Coming from a culture of entitlement, that's a change of revolutionary magnitude. Your employer owes you nothing.*

Trends to ponder as you position yourself for the future:

1. Small and medium-size companies are the engines of job creation. Small companies will be handling the work outsourced by the giants. New technology lets the nimbler and more innovative of the companies compete against the giants better than ever before. Become familiar with smaller companies within your area of expertise. Your future may be brighter there.

2. Even after downsizing is carried to its illogical extreme, **corporate giants probably will not go back to hiring large masses of long-term employees.** They will think it more efficient and profitable to operate as an outsourcing contracting center. Although many corporate leaders, such as Charles Wang, CEO of Computer Associates, disagree with the outsourcing concept, believing that it gives control of one's business to those who aren't invested in it, most corporations have or will begin an outsource for non-core or non-sensitive functions.

The big corporation of the future will consist of a small core of central employees, with a mass of smaller firms working for it under contract. Even within the central core, there will be continuous shifting around and hiring of people for specific, temporary assignments. If you are flexible and have good skills, you may be better off in this new environment than you are now.

Start preparing yourself and your department as if it, and you, were already outsourced. Begin to think like an entrepreneur. Track your income and expenses. Ask daily how you can increase revenue and cut costs. Plan and execute your sales and marketing campaign to let others in the company know about your services. In this way, you can hedge against your departments vulnerability to outsourcing. However, if your department is outsourced and you are offered another position in the company or even laid off, you have the option of starting your own company. Jump start your business by contracting with your former employer as your first customer.

3. Be prepared to work for a foreign company and in a foreign land. Or start that foreign company yourself. Corporations are contracting to have operations carried out at lower cost overseas. For example, New York Life has some claims processing handled by employees in Ireland. Foreign companies investing in American manufacturing are becoming a growing source of jobs. Toyota, Honda and Nissan are hiring workers for their American plants. Mercedes-Benz and BMW will soon join them when they build factories in Alabama and South Carolina. You may increase your chances of working abroad by learning a foreign language. If you work at this language diligently, daily, for only fifteen minutes per day, you can become functionally fluent within a year.

4. Gear yourself toward working for a woman. Women entrepreneurs are starting companies at one-and-a-half times the rate of men. In 1972, three percent of the work force were employed by women, now twelve percent, with the forecast soon twenty-five percent. There are now more new jobs being created by women than by all the Fortune 500 companies :-)

5. Get as much education as possible. The future belongs to the knowledgeable worker. The 55-year-old student is a common campus sight. At Applied Engineering (AE), everyone hired has a college degree, usually in engineering or physics. They spend twenty percent of their time on Research and Development, finding ways to eliminate the manufacturing process that takes the other eighty percent of their time. AE wants their employees to figure out a way to eliminate their jobs, and then they will find better positions for them. If your education does not provide clear bottom-line value to an employer, take classes in those areas that do. People who get paid well in the future will have clear definable skills, and knowledge that immediately translates to profit.

If you are a front line employee, get training in problem-solving, decision-making, teamwork, and interpersonal skills. Learn as many technical and functional skills as you can. If you are a middle manager, learn how to be a good coach and team leader. Learn how to share information effectively, how to take risks, and how to identify and solve customer problems. If you are support staff in finance, planning, audit, human resources, and legal departments, become more flexible with policy change, learn how to perform as facilitator, and how to add value by your performance.

Senior managers and executives would benefit from learning how to make clear performance demands on people, and then hold those people accountable, as well as identifying and remove their own obstacles to performance. All managers need to learn how to use their own time, how to tell the truth, and how to listen.

6. Keep upgrading your skills. Expect to change careers–not just jobs—three or four times during your working life. For example, a high-technology worker needs to upgrade skills every five to ten years. Keep your resume current. These steps do not imply decreased loyalty to your current employer; they simply mean being prepared. Many of the fastest growing preferred positions do not require a college degree but they do require education. The good news is that all the skills required by the new technologically-driven organizations can be learned at community colleges, apprenticeship programs and with on-the-job training. Many programs are government supported.

What you earn depends on what you learn.

Middle managers without discernible, bottom-line skills are losing jobs two or three times faster than one would expect, while professional and technical jobs are being created fifty percent faster than they are cut. **What matters is what you do, not for whom you do it.** Below are listed several skill options to help you position yourself for the future.

Option 1: Finance. Finance is the core of so many companies that no aspirant can afford to avoid schooling in it. Master the math you hated in high school. This will help you understand, among other things, how your company raises and allocates capital. It will also make clear why that new product your team has designed might not be launched. Some of the most talented and valued corporate officers are the new breed of financial officer.

Option 2: Accounting. Managers who know how to read a balance sheet or a profit-and-loss statement are at an advantage. If you're not among that group, sign up for a course in these fundamentals.

Option 3: Computers. The basics of word processing and spreadsheets are essential; how to navigate the Internet is becoming essential. If the best you can do is run the spell checker on your word processor, it's time to update. Be able to set up home pages on the World Wide Web and create interactivity among and between them.

Option 4: Sales and Marketing. Learn how to target a market, capitalize on brand equity, position a product, and use market research techniques.

Option 5: Communication. Technical expertise will get you further if you can express yourself to customers, colleagues, journalists, and the public.

According to William Bridges in *Job Shift* (Addison-Wesley, 1994), we will have several different sources of income from several different skill sets in the employment scenario of the near future. Instead of identifying with your job or your profession, spend the time to identify your skills and values. Very few people have taken the time to identify these. When a job loss or change does occurs, they feel their identity being pulled out from underneath them along with the external reality.

Although your skills and values may be clear to you, many of us meander through life without taking the time to be clear about them. It is extremely important that your identification of self be very solid around values (what is important to you, your mission or meaning), and skills (all that you are able to do), and less around profession or job. For example, a Registered Nurse is a highly-skilled professional who, because of health-care reform, has been forced to re-think his or her professional definition. The old thinking is "I am a registered nurse in the Critical Care Unit." The new thinking is "I value helping others and creating health. My skills are in observation, rapid deductive and inductive thought capacity, scanning, intuition, ability to learn, maintain, enhance, and use of highly technical knowledge, quick mental reflexes, an understanding of networks and systems, interest in teaching, and healing." If this nurse needs to give up the title of nurse and a job in patient care, what do her values and skills allow her to do? Become a case manager? Healthcare network facilitator? Consultant? They are all equally valid as ways of using the described already developed gifts, values and skills.

What are Your Skills and Values?

There are several initial steps to identifying your skills and values, but these are some of the simplest:

Think of what you enjoy doing the most. Make a list of the top three:

1. _____

2. _____

3. _____

Think about what you loved to do as a kid. Write or draw it here.

_____

_____

What do you stand for? One thing willing to die for?

_____

_____

Ask yourself: Who really wants me to work at the job I am now? What did people early in life advise you to do? What was important to your parents? Was it education? Appearances? Wealth? Are your occupations and relationships reflecting this? Is this what *you* want?

_____

_____

When you procrastinate, what do you do? Often, this is what you have talent or deep interest in doing, and can more easily develop into a passion. Write down a couple of suggestions to turn this procrastination into a career or useful pastime.

_____

_____

Ask your friends or colleagues what they think your natural talent is. My friends tell me that my natural talent is:

_____

_____

Imagine your life on video as it appears five years from now, after you have settled into your new lifestyle. Your risk is realized. You are living out your dream. When you can let your video run for a few minutes without extinguishing it with the judgments and limitations you place on yourself, you will feel pride instead of fear connected with it. These exercises will help draw you toward self actualization.

Complete these sentences, each of which will help you focus on your natural wishes and talents:
Someday I would really love to ....
If I could, I would ....
I have always wanted to ....
Wouldn't it be wonderful if I ....

> *Do not complain that you can not see the sunset.*
> *Build your house with windows facing west.*
> Old Proverb

How To Keep Your Job

Perception is all there is. Take charge of building the right perceptions. You start as an expense item at the beginning of the day. By the end of the day, what have you added as value? You must add value and communicate that value in a way that is perceived in order for it to be retained.

Promote Yourself
Make yourself indispensable. You are in charge of building perceptions about yourself. People know little about you and much of that information may be inaccurate. Constantly inform people about yourself and your product.

Push your Ideas Through and Get Credit for Them
Many hate to self-promote because it's 'self centered,' it's not in keeping with their professional image, or they feel they shouldn't have to. They think, "If I'm excellent and work hard, they'll notice and reward it." Many of us work hard, put in long hours and then wake up in mid-career and realize there's no snooze alarm on our biological clocks, the Marlboro man died of cancer, Snow White was a snow job, we're not as effective as we'd like, and our positions are in jeopardy.

❏ If you're blocked just ahead, go through someone else.
❏ Find allies within your company who will support your ideas.
❏ Think through your idea thoroughly before presenting it. Why is the idea good? How does it fit in with corporate strategy? Is it worth the risk and cost?
❏ What resources and skills does the company need?
❏ Never ask for a decision larger than the one you need.
❏ Undercommit and overperform.

Look for the troublemakers
Peter Drucker

*All progress is the result of
unreasonable men and women.*
George Bernard Shaw

Be Mature
Even if you have skills, position yourself well in the company, you can still derail. Moving through corporate ladders and chains requires more. You might also want to show that you can get along with people. These skills are marks of maturity:

a. Accept responsibility. Only the pope is infallible, and then only occasionally. If you've made a mistake, admit it; you'll be admired, not rebuked. Don't try to shift blame to someone else, a sign of immaturity.

b. Let others be right. Coworkers won't tolerate you for long if you have a high need to be right. or if you tell them, "I told you so" or "Why didn't you take my advice?" State your opinion as opinion, not as fact.

c. Trust. Business runs on trust; prying into other people's business and casting doubt on their motives and intentions wrecks trust. Give others the benefit of the doubt. Create trust by doing what you say you'll do.

d. Give first. Show a willingness to help others before you can expect others to help you.

e. Support others' accomplishments. Habitually slighting those around you makes you appear a jealous person, whose judgment can't be trusted. Supporting others will, in the end, support you. As Zig Ziglar has said "If you help enough other people to get what they want, you will get what you want too." Send compliments up as well as down. When someone on does an outstanding job, make sure the employee knows it—and make sure your boss knows it as well. If you are acting in a management capacity, celebrate employee's small successes. Note small things that people do right, and congratulate them at the moment they do them.

> *If you know these things and don't do them,*
> *then you don't really know them. Start doing them.*
> *The road to hell is paved with good intentions.*

f. Don't get caught in a triangle. Triangles are discussed more than once in this book because of the absolute power they have to stagnate any organization. A triangle is an attempted collusion in communication, wherein one individual Person A, tries to ally with another, unsuspecting individual, Person B, against a third individual, Person C. The purpose of it is to strengthen the passive posture of Person A by getting sympathy and support from Person B, and to avoid the responsibility of confronting Person C, who presents as a threat to

Person A.Triangles not only sap the life out of a person, department and company, if you are caught in Position B, you can and will be held accountable and ostracized as if you were the originator of the triangle.

If someone approaches you with a triangle, tell this colleague that you certainly see how tough the situation is for him or her, but that you aren't comfortable listening. Suggest that your colleague speak directly to the other person, rather than forming a habit of speaking to you about a situation over which you have no control. If the matter is important enough, but your coworker doesn't want a confrontation, recommend a talk with the person's supervisor.

If You Have Re-Organized

If you have experienced a recent re-organization, or several of them, here are some suggestions for how to refocus your energies to adapt to the new system.

a. Find out your company's new priorities, and re-align your job responsibilities to them. Stop doing work that doesn't pay off for you or the company, such as busywork, unneeded steps, and duties that contribute nothing. Only you can make these changes.

b. Take on new responsibilities that are also high payoff for you. The challenge of doing them may offset the burnout you experience from overwork. If you *are* becoming burned out, **try to keep committed anyway.** Your commitment is a gift to yourself, not just your company. It helps nothing if you pull back to 50% effort, because your lack of involvement will infect everything you do. If you can't give 100% effort, cut back on what you do, not on the percentage effort with which you do it.

c. If you think you'll find a company that works you less than yours, **happy hunting.** There are constant changes in every company, not just yours. If your organization wasn't under a lot of intense pressure, it wouldn't be surviving.

d. **Don't wait for someone else to make things clearer,** easier, or to lighten your pressure. Pressure is increasing, not decreasing. Take steps to organize yourself. Create clarity in your own work area: you know your company's vision. Create the steps you need to take to make it get there.

e. If you feel your company doesn't care, you may be off-track in your focus. It's not that they don't care, they are doing what they're doing to survive. If you blame someone else, or feel like a victim, move off it. **It doesn't help your job situation, or your well being, to be negative.**

f. **Your company has to change fast.** The more people head in the same direction, the faster the change. When your company makes a decision, practice switching fast instead of digging in your heels. As Warner Erhard has said: "Ride the horse in the direction it's going."

How to Survive Merger Trauma

Anyone involved in a merger wonders: What will the new management expect? How do they measure performance? Will I fit in its culture? How independent will we be? And most of all, should I start looking around? As someone once said, "If your company has been acquired, it gives you an inkling of what it was like to be a slave when you woke up in the morning, and your ownership had changed."

Do some research. What's your new parent's strategy and style? Which product areas are growing and which are being phased out? Why did the company buy you? IBM certainly doesn't need Lotus's facilities, but it needs its technical expertise, which means it needs Lotus's people.

Simplify. This is a stressful time, so maybe you should put off making major purchases and cut back on other major changes in your life. Although the human can tolerate an unlimited amount of change, change over which you cannot predict or control extols much energy and requires tremendous reserves.

Don't expect a smooth transition and quick answers. People assume that when a merger's announced, that there's a plan in place. The reality is, pre-merger activity typically focuses on financials only; don't expect that there is a plan. Thus, decisions to shift people and positions are muddled through following the announcement.

Don't play it safe. Always be ready to leave.

Prepare for Job Loss

Regardless of how much power you think you have, the corporate climate has changed so much that it's reasonable to expect that you can lose your position overnight. However, rather than to live in fear, there are some exercises that might make the prospect of job loss less painful.

Fear of job loss has begun to create a paralysis across North America that makes the loss more likely. Job loss is not failure. Even if it is perceived as such, failure is not the end but rather the beginning. As Henry Ford has said: "Failure is the opportunity to begin again. You will do it better and different this time." Because fear thrives with the unknown and dwindles with knowledge, anything that you can do to prepare for a job loss eventuality can help. These are exercises that others have found helpful to reduce the fear:

 a. Get paid at least once for a skill or hobby outside your current job. It's easy to feel trapped by the job market, worry about how you would ever find something else that pays, and feel overwhelmed by the competition. However, everyone has marketable skills such as writing, speaking, consulting, designing or sales.

The package we create provides the income that we make.

As pointed out earlier in this chapter, identify the skills you could turn to over the next six months if you needed to. Attempt to win at least one client for your services. Psychologically, it is important that you are paid: when you have done it once, you believe you can do it again.

b. Live well below your income for a month. If you needed to, you probably could live on 20% to 25% of your current standard of living, excluding housing, Though you don't need to sell your house as part of this exercise, otherwise budget and live at 25% of your current income. Typically, the large expenses that need to be cut are the ones that you took on to prove to others that you could afford them, not the ones that give you joy. Many folks find after this exercise that they begin to want to give up status objects and appearances.

c. Liquidate on paper everything you have: house, car, equipment, investments. Call a real estate agent in a town or city with a major university and less expensive living costs. You'll find that to rent a good townhouse costs very little. Apply 40% of your liquidated assets to your living costs. You can live many years an acceptable lifestyle in a good community. with the other 60%.

Being trapped by money is psychological. We are programmed to achieve to please others, so we're convinced that external symbols of success are what draw people to us. Many people who were the center of attention one day, were shunned later because they suffered major reversals. This identity fear is the central issue I see in executives contemplating merging or selling their companies, and executive succession.

Those who can see the bridges can cross them more easily.
**People who visualize alternatives
handle transitions more easily.**

d. Ask your spouse and kids to list the things that they like and don't like about you, and how you could improve your relationship with them. They won't mention your job or your money. You'll hear your spouse tell you he would like you to be his partner. You will hear your family tell you that they want to know more of you, have more time with you, feel more loved by you, and that they want to see you happier and more relaxed. Keep their lists and read them whenever you need to comfort yourself that if you lost everything, they will love you anyway.

e. Write a long glowing obituary; what you would like your mother, father or your favorite teacher to read about you. Think about when you are gone and what you would like it to say, not what it would say today given the life line you are currently following.

As Lily Tomlin put it: "The trouble with the rat race is, even if you win it, you are still a rat." Your life is not your career. Change your perspective. Your career should be about living your life *your* way, or as Dewitt Jones, National Geographic Photographer, has said "Make your life your art." The world cannot take away anything unless you give it the power to do so by making the external world your source.

If You And Your Job are Separated
Consider whether or not you could be a consultant if you found yourself between paid positions. Even if this scene is inapplicable to you, preparation to become a consultant is a valuable exercise to sharpen skills and focus talents.

You may do well as a consultant if you:

❏ have a deep understanding of a product, service, job, or industry, even better if this knowledge/experience is in demand or is unique
❏ have been exposed to many different work environments, or one or two in detail
❏ have participated in, or observed, the formation and implementation of business decisions
❏ are self-motivated and can work without an external stimulus.

When you are sure of the change or of leaving your job, following are steps to consider:

a. Rather than focus on job experience, **take stock of your values and skills.** Develop them and list examples of them.

b. Join your professional association. Associations are our modern guilds. Not only will you be able to connect with others for future referrals, your association is up-to-date on developments in your area of experience and can guide you to more resources within your company or town.

c. Computerize yourself. If you are trying to stay hidden until this computer trend passes, you may be missing out. Much of our communication and commerce is, and will, occur electronically. If you are not current with technology, the perception of you will be, firstly, that you are outdated. Secondly, any position you hold in the future will very probably require some expertise with technology. Third, one of the fastest growing areas of opportunity is in helping customers become techno-literate and establish an Internet presence.

d. Put out the word that you are going out on your own. Personal contacts within your industry are a proven source of customers. **Publish articles in trade journals and periodicals.** This is not as daunting as it first seems. Write or call for samples of journals in your area, and request author's editorial guidelines. Browse through existing articles. Follow the style you see, and submit your own version. You may want to call the editor first to see if your article would fit, but my experience is that most editors are grateful for new material and will welcome your article. Once you are published, you are, rightly or wrongly, an expert.

f. Give speeches to conventions, trade associations, and service clubs. Join Toastmasters and finish the first level of competency. Call local Rotary, Kiwanis, and Lions clubs to offer a program on a useful business topic.

g. Send out press releases to trade and local papers. One interview can earn lots of mileage. There is a book of media contacts for most towns, and a book of national media contacts in your local library.

h. Keep moving, challenging yourself, and planting seeds. Success takes time.

Summary:
We are responsible for our own careers, regardless of the actions of the company for whom we work.There are numerous options outside our current level of thinking. Develop focus away from your 'job,' and toward your skills.

 Look back over the notes you've made in the margins in this chapter. Condense them into two action points; two changes you will make as a result of reading this section.

Actions to take:

1._____

2._____

Chapter Nine
Coping with Tomorrow

Asked what workforce changes they consider vital to business success, 519 human resource respondents at a 1995 American Management Association conference placed *adaptability* at the top.

Workforce Characteristic	Percent of Respondents Ranking Trait No. 1
1. Adaptability/greater openness to change	23
2. Ability to see the "big picture" and tailor actions to organizational goals	13
3. More teamwork	12
4. Greater focus on bottom-line financial results	11
5. Greater productivity	10
6. More initiative/individual sense of responsibility	8
7. Continuous learning	7
8. More creativity/innovation	6
9. Different skills	4
10. More risk-taking	2

Note. These data reflect success in the large corporate environment as judged by Human Resource professionals. Other criteria may be used by upper management, and in highly entrepreneurial companies.

Thus, if adaptability and greater openness to change are thought key elements to success on the future, it may be helpful to understand the steps to increased flexibility. One of the first of these, is the ability to **let go of control**.

Could you become a butterfly? Only if you want to fly so much that you're willing to give up being a caterpillar. If you can recognize that life will be *changed*, not *taken away*, you'll be able to make the transition. If you are unwilling to give up what went before, you would become not a butterfly, only a fat caterpillar. The ability to survive in this competitive economy comes from the ability to let go of what was and adjust to the flow of change. If you fall into a fast moving stream, and continue to kick and scream, you, in essence, are holding on to the past. you are still angry at the moment wherein you fell. That is done, past. The fact is, you fell. Deal with what is. Lie down feet first and let the stream carry you down. At some point, because you're fully focused on the present, you'll recognize an opportunity to get out. That is the ability to let go; we will examine the components of letting go later in this chapter.

A second component of openness to change, is the ability to **be flexible**. Guide dogs are trained to two things: to complete obedience, and to use judgment. Thus, the dog has permission to be disobedient when the master's life is in danger. When a sight-impaired person walks out into a busy intersection, a dog has to engage one or the other action. He uses judgment, sinks his teeth into his master's leg, his master gets the message, and returns to the curb. Have you ever seen a guide dog sitting back on the edge of the curb leafing through the policy manual to try to find what to do? We will examine the components of flexibility later in this chapter.

A third component of openness to change, is the ability **to organize information**. If you are overburdened, changes are that you are too exhausted to be open to anything other than retiring on a warm beach. If your desk is piled with paper and you're buried under projects, you may not need time management: you may need to slow down and practice space man-

agement. According to Jeff Davidson, author of *Breathing Space* (MasterMedia, 1991), there are five 'mega-realities' that are causing a glut of information and paper:
1. Population growth.
2. An expanding volume of knowledge.
3. Mass-media growth and electronic addiction.
4. The paper-trail culture.
5. An overabundance of choice.

The following symptoms may reflect information overwhelm:

❑ Talking about not keeping up with what's going on around you.
❑ Feeling guilty about the stack of magazines to be read.
❑ Nodding your head knowingly when someone mentions a book or a news story of which you've never heard.
❑ Finding that you are unable to explain something that you thought you understood.
❑ Blaming yourself for not being able to follow the instructions for putting a bike together.
❑ Refusing to buy new equipment because you are afraid you won't be able to operate it.
❑ Feeling inadequate because you don't know what all of the buttons are for on your VCR.
❑ Buying high-tech electronics because you feel that through osmosis you'll become more literate.
❑ Using your digital watch to log in the exact time to the second even though no one really cares.
❑ Giving time and attention to news that has no cultural, economic, or scientific impact, or no redeeming value.
❑ Being compelled to fill every blank on a form.
❑ Thinking that others understand everything you don't.
❑ Being too embarrassed to say "I don't know."
❑ Calling something information that you don't understand.

According to Richard Wurman in *Information Anxiety* (Doubleday, 1989), **very little of what we take in is valuable information.** There are several situations likely to induce information anxiety: not understanding information, feeling over-whelmed by the amount of information that exists, not know-ing *if* certain information exists, not knowing where to find information, and knowing where to find the information, but not being able to access it.

People have lost the ability to control the flow of informa-tion. We used to have to make a conscious decision to look for information, and to take action to find it. Now, the equip-ment of the information age transmits information without the permission of the receiver. We are vulnerable to the inva-sion of information; it intrudes in our lives, uninvited.

The speed with which it is possible to collect information out-dates most projects before they have been completed. The telephone, the fax, and the various express mail services, by their nature, take away our power of refusal. They change the information that is presented to us, without understanding what each form means to the nature of the information. Although e-mail gives us some right of refusal, few exercise the option. Quality can suffer; phone conversations are inferi-or to talking face-to-face. We are deprived of the nonverbal signals that add to the richness of communication—eye con-tact, facial expressions, hand gestures, and body language.

To regain control is simpler than most people think:
1. Simplify. *In Living the Simple Life: A Guide to Scaling Down and Enjoying More* (Hyperion, 1996), Elaine St. James advises to:

1. Get out of debt, and live on less (*so easy to say*).
2. Have a life that allows you to see more of friends and family.
3. End clutter, all those objects you need to dust, insure, and worry about.

2. Start small. Turn off the TV. Cancel call-waiting. Use only one credit card. Eliminate junk mail. If you don't use it, or

> **Modern Work Life**
> *You can't do it all.*
> *You can't even do more in less time.*
> *Do less in less time.*

can't get to it, don't feel guilty. Throw it out or hide it.

Don't even try to keep up, because you can't. Not knowing something doesn't decrease status, it can increase it if you can admit it. Let new information invade you only if you truly need it. Don't let information in randomly. Avoid bulletin news; watch a longer in-depth format. Reduce exposure to hypercharged media. Don't listen to TV or radio news while dressing for work or commuting. ignore news coverage of spectacular events that don't directly affect you. How many redundant newspapers and magazines do you really need? What's important gets reported everywhere. Clear your world of unimportant low-level decisions that invade mental space. Protect yourself from exploding knowledge. Turn off your information receptors at least part of every day. One day a week, don't read anything. Drop out of the losing battle to 'know it all.' Be ruthless. Make every piece of paper in your office justify itself (Davidson,1991).

> *Information technology exists in the realm of quantum physics. Microprocessors double in price-performance every twelve months. Instead of reaching a point of diminishing returns, products of the information age race toward a vanishing point of infinite power and zero cost.*
> Richard Karlgard

See, you will never keep up–don't try.

3. Reduce Sensory Overload. Set up files in advance for information you will be accumulating, instead of having loose papers hanging about. Decide what should be on your desk, near it, and in it: on top, only computer equipment, a telephone and a few frequently used items. When reading, copy or tear important pages out of magazines, newsletters and reports. Get rid of the rest. Don't hoard magazines or newspapers. You won't miss anything. Scan stuff into a computer if you can. If you can't, buy a scanner. Limit your memos/letters to a third of a page. Use both sides of the paper. Once a quarter, have another look at everything in your work area and practice 'creative trashing.' (Davidson, 1991). Every visual element in your surroundings is recorded in your cortex and lower (survival) brain. Choose carefully.

4. Stop Waste and Inefficiency. There is no wall high enough nor moat wide enough to protect you from inefficiency. According to the Boston Consulting Group, things 'happen' less than 5% of the time in sloppy corporations; the remaining 95% is waste. One of the greatest time wasters and inefficiencies are meetings. Traditional meetings give the appearance of work, but often are a busy way of wasting time where, typically, nothing of real value is accomplished.

 Meeting Guides

1. Don't hold the meeting unless forced. Attend only if you must.
2. Start and stop on time. Don't wait for latecomers.
3. Everyone comes prepared, no excuses.
4. Stop when the agenda or time runs out, whichever comes first.
5. Meet for no longer than 90 minutes. Best length is 45 minutes.
    Stretch every 20 minutes.
6. Make a timed agenda, and stick to it.
7. Appoint a timer who keeps the agenda on time.
8. Appoint a tracker who keeps the meeting on track. Put off-track items into a 'bin.' Allow ten (10) minutes at the end of the meeting to deal with these.
9. Don't let meetings be interrupted.
10. Summarize at the end. Ask for feedback. Outline action items, responsible parties, and follow-up dates.
    Don't table items unless forced–do it or ditch it.
11. Send minutes within 24 hours.
12. Don't be boring. A mind is a terrible thing to waste.

Conventions for the future are changing in requirements as well. At the new wave convention or larger meeting,

❒ Arrange for more interaction time. With our virtual community reducing interpersonal contact, build in more personal contact and networking. Old-style learning where speakers address passive audiences is fading fast.

❒ Sprinkle your meeting with built-in conversation groups and hands-on learning activities. Use technology to increase interactivity.

❒ Update audience seating. If you must have rows, re-shape them to semi-circular, which affords more visual interaction. Put the stage in the middle of the room with steps all around instead of the old classroom-style teacher-at-the front.

❒ Plan frequent attention-shifters. Attention fades at 20 minutes, and leaves at 90 minutes. Many industry speakers with poor visuals can lose your audience fast. Because people can't afford to bore today's audiences, professional speakers are in increased demand. :-)

❒ Make learning surroundings interesting. Contrary to popular thought, adults aren't distracted by interesting surroundings, but may learn even more. Don't close people up in dark, windowless rooms.

5. Develop 'future' skills.
    a. Follow your intuition. Intuition is a sophisticated form of pattern recognition based on experience and training. Because we can't explain it, many organizations don't trust it. That's a mistake, because sterile analytic tools companies use will never guide them into a successful future. A shoe company, for example, wants to decide what new style of women's shoe to make. The company could reach one sort of decision by studying market analysis. It could reach an entirely differ-

ent—and probably better—one, by going to shoe stores, listening to customers' comments, and putting themselves into the shopper's shoes.

b. Understanding. Change isn't a one-time event; it has undercurrents and aftershocks. Even though change can be simple and clear, repercussions can cause more turmoil than the original event because repercussions are unmonitored and unexpected. Don't underestimate even simple changes. When humans confront any change, the uncertainty around the change causes self-criticism, especially when there is a struggle to understand the change. People become self-critical when they have trouble with things, and people who blame themselves when they aren't at fault become nonproductive. Even a simple upgrade of a computer program can create these repercussions. Stick around until the aftershocks are completed, clarify changes such that false interpretations are minimized, and reassure workers that they are doing alright. Be patient with yourself.

c. Flexibility and Resilience. Flexibility is to ability to adjust, make compromises, adapt to new surroundings, and learn new skills. Don't say no to any new idea or change. Ask questions, try it out, and wait. After the dust settles, you may find that it is a positive change. Resilience is the ability to thrive, while wrestling with change, uncertainty and ambiguity. The twin lions that guard the gates of Eastern temples represent confusion and paradox. If we want true wisdom, we need to pass through both. The first step to this wisdom consists of the knowledge of not knowing. Paradoxically, when you're clear about something, that's the next belief system you have to give up. The clearer it is, the more attached you are to its trap. If you're confused and uncertain, you're probably making terrific changes. A system that is off-balance is growing.

> *It's not what you don't know that bothers me;*
> *it's what you know that ain't so.*
>   Will Rogers

d. Patience. Getting out of a stuck place, or changing from your current state is like getting a car out of deep snow. If you gun the engine and power out, you spin tires, and go deeper into the snow. Instead, rock back and forth. Don't rush through. Use impasse time to re-align yourself. When you reach a personal impasse or plateau time, don't push it. Allow it to work through.

> *People reach an impasse,*
> *just before they cure themselves.*
> Fritz Perls

e. Tolerate Ambiguity and Failure. Be able to risk loss and failure. Ontario Hydro under Maurice Strong and Alan Kupcis were willing to take a CDN$1 billion loss in 1993 to restructure, just as AT&T's Bob Allen was willing to take a $1.2 billion loss in 1988 to convert analog to digital transmission. The best of stormscopes or ground radar can't pick up embedded thunderstorm cells, and the best surfer can't predict when a clean up set will wipe out everyone.

> *Pursue risk until you screw up. To be not pushing the limit*
> *in a fast-moving environment is to be falling back.*
> *The thought of going to the grave having been boring*
> *is much more terrifying than the thought of going to the*
> *grave $10 million in debt. There are worse things in life.*
> Tom Peters

f. Clarity. An unclear sense of purpose and vague corporate goals undermine employee productivity. The *Capitol Hill Weekly* diagrammed an explanation by President Reagan concerning knowledge about certain details of the Iran-Contra affair. The President said, "Since I was not informed—as a matter of fact, since I did not know that there were any excess funds until we, ourselves, in that checkup after the whole thing blew up, and that was, if you'll remember, that was the incident in which the Attorney General came to me and told me that he had seen a memo that indicated there were more funds." Information turns into communication when it successfully imparts an idea, not just when it is delivered in a pleasing manner.

> *"What's the use of their having names,"*
> *the Gnat said, "if they won't answer to them?"*
> *"No use to them," said Alice, "but its useful to the people*
> *that name them I suppose. If not why do things*
> *have names at all?"*

Accuracy or facts do not necessarily make things understandable, either. Our five or six-digit diagnostic system doesn't help us understand emotional disturbance or mental health. Data become information only after careful thought and analysis. Whether a plane is at 32,000 feet or 32,112 doesn't add to to experience of flying. In business, although an accountant needs exact figures, she can present sales projections with round offs. Just because technology exists to provide accuracy to the nth degree doesn't mean that we have to take advantage of it. Extreme detail can prevent you from seeing the bigger picture.

> *The illiterate of the future are not those who can't read and*
> *write, but those who can't learn, unlearn, and relearn.*

Control Worry
A frequent response to change is worry, or thought overload. We think in the future in an effort to control it ... but the only effect is deterioration of the present. Worry represents an issue important to you, so an effective strategy would *not* be to try to 'forget about it.' Instead, control it psychologically, by organizing and limiting its strength to control you. Here's an effective worry control plan originated by Thomas Borkovec, Ph.D. from Pennsylvania State University.

Fix a 30-minute worry period at the same time and place every day. Monitor your worries, and identify them when they start. Postpone your worry as soon as you notice it.

Then, attend to the task at hand. Make use of your worry period to worry intensely. If you now worry randomly for a few minutes at a time, worry incubates until you're constantly worrying. When you focus completely, at least you may solve the worries.

Optimism or the Rose-Colored Glass
In these days of constant change, loss, saturation with negative news, and lack of support, pessimism can quickly demoralize the workplace. To help combat this onslaught of pessimism, it may be helpful to know that both pessimism and optimism build on reactions to small everyday events. Pessimism can be coached toward optimism by changing these reactions to events.

> *The ultimate function of prophecy*
> *is not to tell the future but to make it.*

Pessimists respond to unwanted events with a permanent (it will always be this way) and complete (this terrible failure affects all of them) reaction, for example: "Why me? This happens all the time! I'm no good at anything! I never will be. It'll never get better. The world's a mess. People are bad. It's hopeless. May as well give up." All events are then filtered through this pessimistic screen, and hope is virtually impossible. Because this 'belief virus' is quickly spread to others, individual attempts to stamp it out are crucial. Optimism, on the other hand, is realistic, not positive, thinking. To build optimism, practice these new automatic responses:

Keep Focused on Reality and Action.
When unwanted events happen, choose your initial response with care. Instead of anger, move on. Seligman (1990), has found that optimistic, non-depressed persons have:

1. Unrealistically positive self evaluations.
2. Exaggerated perceptions of self control.
3. Unrealistic optimism about the future.

The healthy mind distorts reality in a direction that enhances self esteem and promotes optimism about the future.

Avoid all-or-nothing thinking. Think in percentages: "This happens only x% of the time, not all the time." "It involved only x% of me, not all of me." "It involved only x% of the people of the world, not everyone."

> *Optimism spreads almost as quickly as pessimism.*
> *It takes only one determined optimist to help change the*
> *workplace atmosphere.*

Its not external events, changes in your industry, country, world, it's what you choose to focus on that predicts your success.

The ability to not know, or be confused.

Since males, more than females, may use knowledge as a source of status and power (Tanner, 1990), ambiguity and uncertainty may be doubly stressful for men. Many men in their scramble to keep up, and to give the appearance of keeping up, find it hard to admit that they don't know, and to ask for help. Thus, they can more easily become overwhelmed and derail.

> *Get excited about what you don't know.*
> Dan Burrus

Infomania is the idolizing of facts, which may help in feelings of power, control and superiority. Most of us have been taught since childhood, at least implicitly, to to admit ignorance. 'If you keep your mouth shut, the world can only suspect that you are a fool. If you open it, they will know for sure.' We live in fear of our ignorance being discovered and spend our lives trying to put one over on the world. Ignorance should be an inspiration to learn instead of an embarrassment to conceal.

The refusal to admit to ignorance hampers us every day in our personal relationships and professional development. Collectively, it bears primary responsibility for the anxiety and frustration of staying informed. It also partly explains why the subject is often neglected by those most directly involved in the delivery of information—the communications industry.

The issues related to ignorance and understanding are so highly charged, ephemeral, and subjective that, human nature being what it is, we are all easily distracted from the intangible toward more imminently solvable, corporeal concerns. It simply is easier to conceive of building a new corporate headquarters than creating a new corporate philosophy.

The Ability to Deal with Failure

> *Our aim must be to make our*
> *successive mistakes as quickly as possible.*
> Karl Popper

One reason change is resisted, is the fear of failure. Once failure is experienced, however, often fear abates. More importantly, growth becomes possible. For every real growth, there has been a failure. A butterfly emerges when it's cocoon fails, a lobster grows when it's shell fails. The ability to welcome and let it pass is central to forward movement. If you're not failing occasionally, you're not changing and growing, thus, not adapting. When you 'fail,' view it as only an outcome, learn what you can, correct it the next time around. Failure gives you a chance to try again, and to do it better. Without failing, you could be stuck in life-long mediocrity. Which is the better option?

> *Failure shows that you can take risks. The way people*
> *deal with things that go wrong is an indicator of*
> *how they deal with change.*
> Bill Gates, Microsoft

One of Johnson & Johnson's bases for success lies in their ability to let go of failing units before they become leaden monkeys. Conversely, inability to let go when needed is one of the top predictors of business failure.

21st Century Thinking

1. Thinking in the Gray

> *Eat an apple. Where does it become a non-apple?*
> *Fuzziness is grayness. Atoms assemble and*
> *dissemble a quark at a time.*

We have faith in black and white, the bivalence of Western thought can be traced back to the Greeks. In Aristotle's binary logic, it is either *A* or *not A*. The sky is *blue* or *not blue*. This was philosophically correct for over 2000 years. Buddha, who lived in India almost two centuries before Aristotle, broke through black and white thinking and saw world of contradictions. According to Kosko (1993), Einstein himself doubted the mathematical framework of the black and white science that he helped to build:

> *So far as the laws of mathematics refer to reality,*
> *they are not certain. And so far as they are certain,*
> *they do not refer to reality.*

Logical positivism was the dominant philosophy of science during this century: if you cannot test, or mathematically prove what you say, you have said nothing. Positivism has worked well for scientists, because it has allowed only them to speak, and for graduate schools who have controlled the thinking of graduate students, who were forced to substantiate all arguments. Whatever thought could not be supported by data, was meaningless.

Everything is a matter of degree.
Making up ones mind may be no more important than learn-
ing how to change one's mind. When exploring the future,
indecisiveness may be the best strategy.
John Krumboltz

2. Thinking in Opposites

Break-through creativity often happens in the spaces in and around things, the silence between friends, the time between the notes of music, the break time during a conference, the space between buildings–negative space. The opposites of things are more interesting than the things themselves.

Look for a solution which has a valid *oppositeness*. Not a *different* way of looking at things, but an *opposite* way. Look at a table with the place settings as the focal points; then look at them as the backdrop for the table. Look at cities the same way. Artists do these figure-ground exercises all the time.

Opposites are what you look at everyday but never really see, or what you expect will never happen, but does. Typewriters were designed with carriages that moved from left to right to accommodate keys that were always struck in the same place. Then IBM asked, "why couldn't the paper stay in the same place and the printing mechanism move across the page?" That question revolutionized office machines. Scientists researched polio from a live virus. The Salk vaccine was developed from a dead virus. Opposites inspire most scientific discoveries and business developments. Looking at opposites is a way of testing an idea to see if it works. It is a way of seeing, listening, and testing.

Interpreting information by asking: "How can I look at this from different or opposite vantage points?" and "How would reorganizing the information change its meaning?" Instead of being bound by the accepted way of organization, what happens if you mix everything up?

The real act of discovery consists not in finding new lands,
but in seeing with new eyes.
Marcel Proust

3. Taking Risks

As a young man explained surfing to me, "You gotta swim
out into the No Fear Zone. It's scary to get right out there
but if you don't, you'll be wiped out. You wait for the last of
the set, like you can see it coming, start moving with it and
then you climb up real fast. You have to make a fast decision.
If it seems good, commit to it 100%. If you don't really commit to it, it will take you in. Don't wait too long, you'll miss
it. Every once in a while, a huge wave comes in called a
"clean-up set," and there's nothing you can do about it. It
takes everybody out. Just go with it, let it take you in, and
then come on back out and wait for the next one." There is
safety inside the waves, but the real fun comes in risking the
big wave, always with the knowledge that you can be wiped
out at any time. That's simply part of the process.*

No man can climb out beyond the
limitations of his own character.
Robespierre

You gain strength courage and confidence from
every experience. You must stop and look fear in the face.
You must do the thing you cannot do.
Eleanor Roosevelt

Summary:

The ability to cope with tomorrow has as much to do with
giving up, as it does with *learning new*. You have the ability
to let go of ways that no longer serve you, of increased flexibility, and of limiting information. You can't keep up, don't
try. Limit yourself to information that you *truly* need. Two

* The reader is referred to *Dancing with Tigers* (Lapp, 1994) which
provides a complete program on risk taking.

future thinking skills are 'thinking in the gray,' and seeing in opposites. A third is the ability to take risks to use these first two skills.

 Look back over the notes you've made in the margins in this chapter. Condense them into two action points; two changes you will make as a result of reading this section.

Actions to take:

1._____

2._____

Chapter Ten
New Age Leadership

Leadership is all about the example we set, not the position we hold. A river never rises above its source, just as our children will never rise above who we are.

Captain James T. Kirk's top-down management style reflected how managers did their jobs 30 years ago. Jean-Luc Picard, captain of the Starship Enterprise, in 'Star Trek, The Next Generation' reflects the leadership style of the future. Jean Luc Picard is a leader. He is somebody everyone can trust and rely on. He isn't going to fight without reason. With a combination of consensus leadership as well as decisive leadership, Picard, even in a crisis, opts for consensus and asks for other people's opinions. Even when the ship is about to blow up, he remains calm and says, "Hey, I need your help here." In other words, what he's saying to his people is that "if you're good enough to be in your position, you're good enough for me to listen to."

Picard doesn't always act on his crew's advice. He still may decide he wants to do what he had originally intended to do. But his people know they'll be listened to.

Picard stresses these leadership qualities:

1. Focus. "If you first focus your efforts on makers of the highest concern ... you will set free ... your crew's and your own initiative, power, innovation and imagination."

2. Urgency. "If you engage each mission . . . with a sense of urgency, you will attain many marvelous accomplishments."

3. Initiative. "It has often been the crew's initiative that has made a difference in the success and safety of our missions.... When you are asked for approval of an action, you should end every reason to respond with Permission granted."

4. Competence. "Becoming a competent officer should be your top priority, using the best tools and information available to break situations into problems and opportunities."

To assess informally *your* leadership skills, ask yourself:

❑ **Do my reports feel important?** A leader helps people believe that what they are doing is significant and meaningful, and that they do make a difference to the group's success.

❑ **Do I value learning and competence?** Encourage your staff to expand their skills. Treat failures and mistakes as opportunities to learn.

❑ **Do my people share a sense of community?** You need to draw people together toward a common goal that overcomes other differences.

❑ **Do my people see the work as exciting?** If your staff perceives the project as exciting and/or important, they'll motivate themselves to get the work done.

Models for leadership are available to us everywhere. The

Ritz-Carlton Hotel Company, winners of the 1992 Malcolm Baldrige Award, have progressed from 30% defects in 1991, to seven percent in 1994, and in 1996 they plan to be defect-free. At least for this company, their Baldrige and TQM efforts seem to be working. One reason for this may be their change leader, President and COO Horst Schulze. These are his recommendations:

1. Be visible and available. Schulze lunches almost daily in the employee's cafeteria and walks his own property several times a day, asking for employee suggestions and comments.

2. Ask, don't tell. Ask the people who do the work what to do and how to do it. Employees I surveyed at each Ritz-Carlton felt empowered to direct the future. Why? They were asked, sincerely listened to, and freed up to make their own decisions. Every employee at The Ritz-Carlton is authorized to spend up to $1500 to correct a guest problem.

3. Communicate the company's direction and destination constantly. At a daily ten-minute 'Line-Up,' all employees receive the message of the day and review the credo. Everyone on board has a map of the journey. At their thorough orientation, employees memorize the Credo, Principles, the Basics and the Three Steps of Service. Continual teaching is carried out by the best employees.

4. Measure and reward people along the way for what you want them to do. At The Ritz-Carlton Company, all desirable behaviors and goals are rewarded in several different ways.

From Horst Schulze:
There are three major areas of resistance to change in a corporation. The first is top management, the second is middle management, and the third is lower management. The employees are never the problem. They not only adapt well, they know what needs to be done and can't wait to do it.

*Move heaven and earth to keep every guest. Each guest can
potentially give you $100,000 worth of lifetime business.
You have to be a complete idiot as a General Manager not to
spend $250 to make any guest happy.*

*Managers don't want to change because they've been doing
it the same old way for 40 years and they need to be right.
Well, they have been doing it wrong for 40 years.*

Another model was the late Sam Walton of Wal-Mart. In
1978, Jack Kahl was making a 6:30 AM sales call in
Bentonville, Arkansas. The client was an up-and-coming discount chain called Wal-Mart. Despite the early hour, the boss,
Sam Walton, was already at work and passed Kahl in the
hall. Instead of a brush-off from Walton, Kahl was greeted
with: "Young man, are we doing enough to serve you at
building our partnership?" Walton wasn't just being flowery.
Partnership was what he *meant*. For Walton, suppliers were
close associates, people who worked with Wal-Mart for
mutual benefit. Sam Walton grew 23% a year, surpassing
Sears in January 1994. He was a fanatic. He gave his phone
number out to everyone. He jumped up on counters to talk to
people. He was inspired and inspiring.

*It was never cost containment that was needed,
but productivity. When the culture is led by executives
who proclaim the journey, the organization receives a
powerful, positive uplift.*

New Wave Leadership Traits
A summary of suggestions for leadership trait development to
serve in the new wave:

1. Get Excited.
Leaders, firstly and above all, are passionate about the future.
If you don't know or care where you're going, get out of the
driver's seat. Bring in a visionary who can see it and get fired

up about it. Telecommunications, Inc.'s COO Brendon Clouston is passionate when he communicates TCI's future to his team. If you're not inspired by yourself and what you have to offer, why should anyone else be?

2. Create a memorable vision.

Leaders make the vision simple, easy to understand and translate it daily, so that all levels can make instant yes-no decisions based on it. Disney created a physical model and placed it in the employee's lounge for all to see. Begin and end each meeting with your vision, and use it in every conversation. Posters and memos don't cut it.

3. Decide where you need to go, not how you're going to get there. Leaders put employees in charge of deciding how change will be implemented because employees understand the culture. Off-the-shelf quality and change programs don't stick because they don't get rooted in your own culture and belief systems. This is the least employed leadership trait but probably the most important.

4. Stick close to the troops.

Fourth, leaders stick close to the troops. At Precor, managers spend a day with service technicians or maintenance persons to experience problems at gut level. Bill Chiles, formerly of SuperCuts, sat in both his own and his competitor's waiting rooms watching and asking questions. Herb Kelleher, CEO of Southwest Airlines, sits up until 3:00 AM with mechanics. Horst Schulze, President of The Ritz-Carlton Hotel Company, lunches in the employee cafeteria.

The main requirements of leadership are guts and judgment. To win trust, you have to make yourself vulnerable. You've got to be out there dealing with real problems, on the front line where people can watch you and personally size you up.

5. Strengthen leadership throughout.

Fifth, leaders strengthen other leaders throughout the organization. Leaders listen to anyone with an original idea, no matter how absurd it might sound at first. Leaders encourage, they don't nitpick. Leaders hire good people, leave them alone, and let them run with ideas. If you have trouble spotting leaders, ask co-workers who are the most admired people and who in the organization tells the truth. They're the leaders.

6. Be interesting.

Sixth, and lastly, leaders care enough about the effect they have on their people to learn to be interesting. The old management style of barking orders, lecturing, and memo-sending worked for the Prussian Army, not for folks of the 90's. Don't be boring, and don't turn your people off. Learn to be charismatic. Charisma persuades people to do things they'd rather not. Others will charge over the hill, run through fire., walk barefoot on broken glass as well as commit to other, less dramatic, changes. Not many people have charisma. But it isn't a mystery. More than charm and personal magnetism, it's the ability to get others to endorse your vision and promote it passionately. Charisma matters more than it used to. When command-and-control environments were acceptable, each person knew his role, and almost automatically executed the boss's program. Today, if you're unable to galvanize people into action, all the thinking, the analysis, the strategic prioritizing doesn't matter.

Below are listed five characteristics of charismatic people, and suggestions on how to develop the trait:

   a. Charismatic people reduce complex ideas into simple messages. They communicate by using symbols, analogies, metaphors, and stories. If they're really charismatic, everyone, –including people on the factory floor, janitors, and hotel housekeeping staff–understand the message. Ronald Reagan, was unwavering on his two core beliefs: a strong defense and less government. Marianne Williamson and Tony Robbins, despite limited education, still have absolute conviction of their beliefs, and both simplify and exaggerate to win charismatic points.

b. They connect and inspire. Leaders are optimists, who like to do things that haven't been done before. Whether they succeed or not, a remarkable thing often happens: Their boldness inspires others. Simply by being in the presence of a charismatic person can inspire boldness in oneself. Charismatic people speak emotionally about putting themselves on the line. They connect with others hearts as well as their minds.

c. They are empathetic. Empathetic people are able to see things from another person's perspective. With the exception of severely disturbed sociopathic individuals, most everyone can develop some empathy for others.

To practice empathy:
a.Think, "If I were the (other person), how would I feel about this?" Studies show that women tend to be more experienced than men at stepping into another's shoes.

b. Make others feel they are the most important people in the room. Never look away when they are speaking to *you*.

c. Reverse roles with someone else and play out various scenes and circumstances.

d. Charismatic leaders *push*. Charismatic leaders follow a set of principles that direct them to what they believe is right, and they challenge and provoke others. Charisma can be a positive or negative force. Pat Buchanan, a 1996 GOP contender, had the absolute conviction of his beliefs, even though these beliefs changed daily. Charlie Manson and Adolf Hitler, both charismatic leaders, had absolute conviction of their beliefs. So did Martin Luther King and Ghandi.

e. Charismatic leaders focus on the emotional issues that connect them with their followers. One trait many memorable leaders share is their ability to communicate values and ideas. Leaders focus on the emotional issues that connect them with their followers. Leaders in the business world always stress values shared by their employees, enlisting their employees on a mission that gives their work purpose and direction. When Lee Iacocca became president of Chrysler, he was able to lead his employees because they knew he shared their values and goals.

A leader communicates vision. By defining the organization's direction and goals, the leader defines the organization's future, becoming a catalyst for change. Not everybody agreed with Ronald Reagan's policies, but no one can deny that he had a clear, definite vision of the country's future.

People learn best by copying what other people do, not what they say. Your employees learn best from what you do as a manager, not what you say. Your employees are treating your customers exactly the way they are being treated by you.

Leaders use a variety of communication techniques. Some write memos, some put themselves on videotape. Hewlett-Packard's president can speak directly to every HP employee in the world via microphone. But all leaders recognize that personal, face-to-face communication is their most effective tool in promoting their organization's values and future.

Beyond the above traits, however, there is no distinctive leadership style that tends to be effective across situations. A good example is a comparison of Eaton at Chrysler, Trotman at Ford and Smith at GM. Each spent his entire career within the auto industry. What's different is how they manage change in different settings with a similar management style. Modesty, self-effacing humor, open discussion, honesty, and team play are all in. Pomp, protocol, pretension and paperwork are out. But does that style get anything done?

At Ford, Trotman has low tolerance when key issues are being debated. He doesn't like nonsense or mystery. He likes to have everyone's cards on the table and get dissent out of the way before they move on. After that, everyone moves together and they don't look back. "We all go for it, very straightforward and simple."

To save the Mustang from the scrap heap, Trotman allowed free reign to a skunk-works operation where teamwork and cooperation replaced procedures and hierarchies. He put engineers and computer designers into the same test cars to keep different technical worlds focused on the real product. Trotman checked up on the Mustang project in after-hours visits by the back door instead of formal briefings.

Eaton arrived alone at Chrysler, brought in none of his deputies, and fired no one. He turned out to be a morale-building coach. He doesn't believe in one-person shows but pushes long and hard for what he thinks is right.

GM's Jack Smith has dropped nearly all the trappings of solemn power including the dining room. Instead of hiding away in his corner 14th-floor suite, Smith spends most of his 14-hour days in his small office 15 miles away, closer to the plants. Smith's management style is already showing through.

The problem was never the people. It was the screwed-up structure we had. We had to change it. It took us years to understand that. You go through a denial phase.

The three chief execs get together for private dinners once a month, ushering in a whole new era of cooperation. They all agree that competition among the Big Three is no longer aimed at creating problems or celebrating each others' misfortunes. Instead, they celebrate each other's successes.

Farkas & Wetlaufer's (1996) article *The Ways Chief Executive Officers Lead* revealed five different styles of leadership that were not based on the leader's personality but rather the demands of the job. That is, effective leaders are able to work outside their own style if needed.

Change for the sake of change makes no sense. But if you're not working for constructive strategic change, then you are the steward of something that must, by definition, erode. Competitors will surpass you, and clients will find you less relevant. If that was your approach to leadership, why would you even want the job?

Change Masters
When Jos Wintermans, former President of Canadian Tire Acceptance Ltd., took over the reins as President in 1988, there were less than 40,000 Canadian Tire card holders. Now there are 800,000. The first retailer with own their own Mastercard, CTAL now has a travel service and auto clubs through the United States, and Puerto Rico. Their insurance division has over a million policy holders. After a recent program for Canadian Tire Acceptance in Niagara Falls, Ontario, Jos and I spoke of his past, how he has accomplished change, and what drives him.

When asked his concerns, he replied: "Not business concerns; business problems are not complex. I feel responsible for people, especially the front line. If I fail, they have no work." Action-oriented, Jos gets things done. "I focus on the how's not the what's, so perhaps I take more action than others." These are two steps Jos took in helping his people to change.

1. Created Urgency
In Jos' words: "I asked, 'is there a future for CTAL?' If we continued as we were, the answer was no, so we had urgency.

Then I took one third of my managers out of operations and sent them to sales and marketing."

2. Established Trust

"Because of position changes, we had violated trust. I held a series of half-day group values sessions with all employees. We asked, 'where are we (and you)?' and 'where do we (and you) want to be?' Personally, can you commit to our values?"

"During the next two years, all my decisions were scrutinized. When our mainframe was moved to the head office in Toronto, and we re-hired everyone who would have lost a job, they saw my commitment. When I fired a top manager on the spot for sexual harassment, they saw my commitment. Commitment has to be visible."

A business is a living organism. There will always be a point where the environment changes, the competition changes, something critical changes, and you must realize this and take the leading role in meeting change.
Edzard Reuter, CEO of automaker Daimler-Benz

One neglected aspect of leadership is the examination of the bond leaders make with their followers. According to Strebel (1997), managers and employees view change differently. Too few leaders recognize how people commit to change. Although top management views the change as ways to enhance both the corporation and their careers, many employees, see change as disruptive and intrusive. This schism can be enough to completely block change efforts. Formal, psychological, and social bonds have been broken, and need to be re-created before employees can buy into changes that alter the status quo. If there is not alignment between a company's statements and management's behavior, change will be undermined. It is difficult to recover management's credibility once lost.

During a Canadian phone utility's prosperous years, a tradition of lifelong employment was part of the company culture.

Job security came in exchange for loyalty to the company and to individual managers. Informal rules and personal relationships dominated formal systems for performance evaluations and career advancement. Managers' job descriptions and position in the hierarchy set limits on their responsibilities, and operating outside those boundaries was discouraged. Subordinates weren't encouraged any differently. People weren't trying to meet challenges facing the company or even looking for personal growth. Position and perceived power in the company network determined who got what. Even when costs were demonstrably out of line and operating margins were declining, the company had no mechanism for holding people accountable for failing to achieve financial targets.

James Collins in *Built to Last,* claims that companies built on belief systems outlast those without them. It's not the content of the beliefs that matters but the fact that they give employees something to work for beyond a paycheck.

New Age Leaders

Leaders have the courage to cut through the jungle brush, unsure of their direction, clearing a path for others, can climb up the tallest tree, and have the supreme courage to call out to all the gathered: "Wrong jungle!" and lead the grumbling and complaining expedition through an entirely different jungle. The policy wonks, sold school human resources people, and legal staff will never be happy with change.

 Look back over the notes you've made in the margins in this chapter. Condense them into two action points; two changes you will make as a result of reading this section.

Actions to take:

1._____

2._____

Chapter Eleven
Guiding Change

Scaring people isn't the answer. You try to appeal to them.
The more they understand why you want change,
the easier it is to commit to it.

Natural systems distribute intelligence outward and reject central authority, controlling from the bottom up (Kelly, 1994). They become complex, not complicated, by creating layers of simplicity; they encourage diversity, eccentricity, instability, maximize fringes, and seek disequilibrium. They don't manage change, they encourage it. They also change how they change. When their organization is centered around these guiding principles, a powerful effect is felt. This chapter examines methods of leadership in the 'natural organization.'

At the end of the day, you bet on people, not strategies.
Lawrence A. Bossidy, AlliedSignal

Involve people
Before implementing change, find out who will be affected by it. Get people's ideas, and even if you can't use them, you'll save considerable resistance later on. The RACI acronym

introduced in Chapter Three may be useful here, as well: who is responsible for this, who has authority over it, who has had control over this in the past, and who else is influenced by it?

R   Who is responsible for this?
A   Who has authority over it?
C   Who has had control over this in the past?
I   Who else is influenced by it?

It's not a platitude to say that you have to use people's brains and imagination and dedication. They know their jobs better than you do. The fellow running the lathe in the factory knows more about that part of the process than the bureaucrat in the office.

√ Who has the greatest stake (gain or loss) in the outcome?
√ Who else will be affected by outcome?
√ Who should be involved in the process?
√ Who should be consulted before the final decision?
√ Who should be informed afterwards?
√ Who should manage the process? Who can benefit the
        most? The person who needs it the most will probably
        do the best job.

As mentioned in Chapter Two, Ford's latest re-organization is working better because the whole company is involved. Past re-organizations were ordered by top management and met resistance. Hyatt employees are encouraged to ask questions concerning orders from the Chicago headquarters, and they rewrite almost three-quarters of corporate edicts. Hyatt's Camp Hyatt and Rock Hyatt are working and have resulted from employee suggestion. Hyatt has helped finance employee startups, sometimes subcontracting work back to them.

Don't wait for consensus
You need critical mass buy-in only. According to Jon Katzenbach in *Real Change Leaders* (Katzenbach, 1996), a critical mass of about 33% is needed. You may need as few as

ten to twelve people in your organization to begin to effect real change. The greatest change bottleneck is to wait for everyone to come on board. They won't. Drag them kicking and screaming into the future. Both consensus-building and bottom-up decision-making slow things down and cost more than they yield. The best decisions often are made by top-down activist managers after consulting and asking for ideas. Mitsubishi, for example, had developed a bottom-up style, where ideas percolated to the top. Unfortunately, ideas were stopped in their tracks by mid-management, and paralysis resulted.

Take time to cover all bases, loose ends, and assignments. Don't tell your decision, sell your decision.Communicate changes in person, and follow up with a brief memo. When you have critical mass, damn the torpedoes and go full speed ahead. Commit to the decision.

> ❏ Involve everyone ... ask people who do the work.
> ❏ Move faster! Correct as you go. You cannot have
> all the details worked out; there is no time.
> ❏ Open up, reveal, inform constantly.
> Tell your people the truth.
> ❏ Manage confusion and fear. You can't remove it.
> Allow for, and respect it.

Reward Carefully

Jeffrey Pfeffer, Professor of Organizational Behavior at Stanford, explains why, despite continual effort, corporations fail to change. A commonly-held human behavior model is that workers don't like to work, and without an external control or incentive, won't perform. This view lacks empirical support. Secondly, the assumed efficiency of hierarchy lingers in business-school theorizing and corporate belief systems. As organizations try to decentralize, the inconsistency paralyzes. Pfeffer cites the example of Macy's, in financial stress after a leveraged buyout. Realizing the importance of employee performance, Macy's insisted on strict attendance rules and higher sales quotas, threatening to fire employees if they couldn't reach them. Not once did Macy's consult their own employees for advice on sales performance. Result? Pickets, grievances, lower sales, poorer performance, rock-bottom morale. Strong external incentives with close monitoring can provoke psychological reactance, a drive to restore control. Increased attempts at hierarchical control will produce attempts to circumvent the control, leading to addition efforts at surveillance, and the organization spirals downward in a wasteful cycle of behavior. If organizations are serious about overcoming serious obstacles that stand in the way of obtaining competitive advantage through people, they need to become more pragmatic, rather than theoretical or ideological, about the employment relationship. which means, understanding the realities of human psychology.

A 1994 survey of United States executives by the firm Robert Half International, revealed that people are more inclined to leave their jobs because of lack of praise and recognition than for money. Forty-six percent of respondents cited 'limited recognition' as the most common reason for leaving an employer, and twenty-nine percent said 'compensation.'

Be Clear
These are times when clarity is needed. Under changing conditions, many managers think they should be more tolerant of employees' behavior. Tolerating inappropriate behavior gives license to that behavior and increases poor behavior. It also makes other employees more anxious and uncertain about who you are and what you stand for.

People need to know the rules of the new game. Without them, things appear illogical and inconsistent. Be clear about the nature of the commitment you make to employees, and the nature of the commitment you expect from employees. Make obligations and expectations overt and clear. Without clarity from the organization, people won't know where they stand, and they'll experience more anxiety than they should. Without a clear position, organizations will make inconsistent decisions that will fuel people's fears.

A reasonable new-wave reasonable commitment is one in which people would earn some form or some amount of security by achievement, predicated on the organization's ability to handle costs of employment. In contrast to the absolute security that created entitlement (Bardwick, 1994), this is contingent security, based on value added. It encourages the development of confidence and courage. Contingent security is probably the condition most likely to develop people who will become comfortable in virtual corporations.

Be clear. If you must fire people, tell it like it is. Don't fudge around with terms like 'forced imbalance,' 'risk,' 'competitiveness,' 'repositioning,' 're-engineering.' They help no-one. Be straight. It makes it easier for everyone.

Set Clear Goals

Make goals and methods transparent enough that your employees will be willing to take some calculated risks. You want hundreds of people making informed choices and taking risks simultaneously. You do not want them all second-guessing each other or wondering if the boss really means what he or she says.

1. Limit the number of goals.
2. Link the program to these goals directly.
3. Focus on core business and ask continually what the changes are doing for your customers. If nothing, avoid making them.
4. Spend a minimum amount of time setting up the program.
5. Start with clear objectives.
6. Who is your customer, what service are you providing and what business strategy are you satisfying?
7. Pay for performance.

Allow Space
Create space and time for your most valuable change asset: the creativity of your people. Hallmark facilities include a creativity center, where employees are given free reign and time to create. RJR Nabisco's SnackWells fat-free cookies and crackers resulted from their innovation push. Hewlett-Packard people have unlimited access to equipment and labs, and are asked to spend 10% of their free time on their own projects. Merck researchers are given time and resources to go after high-risk high-payoff ventures. Hasbro gets ideas from kids they bring in to play in their Fun Lab. Over 30% of General Mills sales are from new products out in the past five years. Each of their cereal brands must be significantly improved every three years or yanked off the shelves.

> *You don't manage invention ... you manage an environment in which invention occurs.*
> John Seely Brown, Chief Scientist, Xerox Corporation

Anxiety improves performance until a certain optimum level of arousal has been reached. Beyond that point, performance deteriorates as higher levels of anxiety are attained. McClelland (1978) found that motivation to achieve and level of effort keep rising until the expectancy of success (or the level of uncertainty) reaches 50 percent. Then, even though the expectancy continues to increase, motivation falls. When the goal is seen as too easy (too certain to win) or too difficult (too certain to fail), there is no motivation or effort.

Stage 1 Organization. Denial or No Change
In Stage One, it is very hard to fire people. Enforcing discipline takes careful justification. Promotion is mostly based on seniority. There are many hierarchical levels. Formal status is extremely important. There is no risk taking but many rules. Lots of paperwork, lots of people checking on others. Many studies and pilot efforts. No new decisions are made. People don't have much energy.

When there is corporate denial, create some tension or urgency. Create significant positive or negative outcomes as a result of performance.

Stage 2 Organization. Snail-Paced Change
Formal position in the hierarchy determines influence. There is some teamwork. Peer pressure is important. Decisions are made by consensus, although with more discussion than in Stage 1. There is time given to analyze and plan. Change is typically thoughtful, logical, and incremental and happens very slowly. The mood is calm, people are somewhat involved. Folks aren't afraid of change, but prefer to study the situation from many different angles before proceeding.

Stage 3 Organization. Progressive Change
There are few levels of hierarchy (four or fewer). Dynamics of most relationships are like those of peers. There are many autonomous teams, few rules, and considerable flexibility. Creativity is rewarded. Evaluations cover the full 360 degree range. There are significant rewards and punishments according to performance. Organization is performance or customer driven. Outcome is much more important than how to do it. Trust is high, and channels of communication are open.

Stage 4 Organization. Unfocused Change
There is discomfort because no one knows the right way to do things. Decisions are pushed upwards to the top. There is much doubt about the future, some skepticism that it can be made to work, some put down of the leadership, but also a glimmer of hope. Some people may be leaving. The pendulum of values moves in wide arcs, because the preference is action. Senior management shows impatience when solutions are not at a high enough energy level. There is a tendency to overreact. Unfortunately, there's so much going on, there's so much coming down, people don't know what's going to happen. People can't let their guard down and they can never let up.

If the mood is anxious, reduce anxiety. Be straight about

what's happening and what people can expect; don't leave room for rumors. Emphasize successes and historic stability.

Stage 5 Organization: Chaotic Change

There is no sense of security or predictability. Leaders are absent. Rules and precedents from the past are not appropriate, but there are no new rules that are clear. There is a lot of floundering. Senior management grabs new rules (or a visions or cultures) from somewhere else rather than let them evolve from within. There is discussion of future goals but the goals or vision of people are discounted. There is poor morale and communication is top-down. Decisions are rarely made, and less frequently implemented. The mood is cynical.

For chaotic organizations, suspend all change efforts and strive for calm and stability.

 Where is
Your company? Your part of the business?
Your supervisor? Your direct reports?
The person at the next desk? Yourself?

Trust in the Organization

Core change can create mistrust, even almost paranoiac conditions in which most of people's energies are used to protect themselves. When this occurs, they are not psychologically available for purposeful actions.

Trust is a fundamental requirement for achievement, decision making, creative disagreements, cooperation, teamwork, and a sense of unity. Ineffective communication creates mistrust. Trust is needed to get people to buy in to new values and accept new processes. The upheaval of major change always threatens trust, because trust is based on predictability.

Trust is created when people are told what's going to happen and it does. By definition, change creates unpredictability and inconsistency. The perception of inconsistency is made worse when the people in control seem to jump from one strategy to another, from one business guru to the next. Instead of generating a sense of hope and trust, and creating excitement in an organization, this inconsistent behavior increases cynicism about the leader effectiveness and decreases trust. Instead of flexibility, this is perceived by people as as the flailing about of desperate management.

An organization is like a pendulum. Upper management is at the top of the pendulum, and most employees are at the bottom. When the pendulum swings, the top remains fixed while the bottom swings in the widest arc. Thus, people nearer the bottom are far more likely than people closer to the top to feel jerked around by things that are out of their control. Thus, trust is harder to create and sustain among that group. This is similar to the phenomenon of crowd communication at the Bay-to-Breakers race in San Francisco each year. As the race starts, the lead racers run out, and slowly the thousands behind them start to move. The distance between the lead racers and those at the tail end is so great that the start of the race is only a rumor for those at the end. It takes a great deal of time before the tail end starts to move. When the tail racers actually finish the race, the lead racers have long ago finished.

Effective communication is both necessary and central to creating trust. In a culture high fear, few messages are sent, and no one 'hears.' There is little real communication, because people either don't know what to say or they're afraid to tell the truth. One of Motorola's ingredients for success is their cult of conflict and open dissent that unearths mistakes, and fixes them quickly. Johnson & Johnson produces more winners than losers with its 'no blame' encouragement of innovation. Some companies celebrate the 'Mistake of the Month.' In this way similar errors are unearthed, learning-from-experience grows, and an atmosphere of trust can grow. The try-something-new mentality could mean added unforeseen successes for your company. The $400 million Post-it notes were an error with glue. Cool Whip was a shaving cream mistake, and Nyquil was a straight cold remedy that knocked testers out.

How to Restore Damaged Trust

A cracked vessel never holds as much water.
Old Czechoslovakian saying

Employees feel deeply betrayed by their companies and managers. According to Princeton Survey Associates, only 38% of workers trust management to keep their promises. How, and if, trust is restored is crucial to employee loyalty, the success of the company, and to society. This is what managers who have restored trust have done. They:

- ✓ kept their word.
- ✓ shared more information than they had in the past and justified job losses with objective data.
- ✓ If employees were to make decisions, management gave them detailed financial information and operations data that helped them link what they did to the overall company goals.
- ✓ established a common set of clear values and spent time getting commitment to them.
- ✓ let people make decisions in their own areas. Gave them the tools they needed to do the job, and didn't undermine them.
- ✓ gave them direction, feedback, and reasons why they were doing the jobs they were.
- ✓ clarified goals and aligned them with a reward system that made sense.
- ✓ helped people develop skills with long-term applicability and value.

Start building trust. Doing what you promise is central to establishing trust. Whether you're dealing with a customer or coworker, listen to what you promise and follow up on it.

If you say:	Be sure you:
I'll get back to you.	Get back to the person.
I'll find out.	Find out.
I'll call her.	Call her.
Take your time.	Give the person time.
I'll try to help.	Try to help.
I'll take care of it.	Take care of it.
What do you think?	Listen to what is said.

Don't Punish Errors. Employees spend a good proportion of time covering up potential errors to protect themselves. Celebrate failure if principals and values were followed. Don't just praise victory. Just as none of us would punish our children if they fell while trying to walk, or jump, or run. With the assumption that our employees are doing their best, errors are simply sources for learning.

How to Develop Trust in Teams

1. Share Goals. Get agreement on goals and make sure everyone has commitment to the group. Agree on the team's vision and purpose: why it exists, where it's going, and what it's trying to do. Commit to the same values: What you stand for, how you define success, what is ethical and fair behavior.

2. Connect to the Larger Organization. Develop team purpose and goals in collaboration with external and/or internal groups such as customers, suppliers, partners, or senior managers. Get the authority needed to do what it is responsible to do. Align the work the team needs to do with the work done in the company.

3. Make sure the organization invests financial, managerial and time resources in the team. Require that top management trust and respect decisions made by the teams.

4. Communicate Clearly

Set up channels for feedback and upwards communication. Setting up an open door policy and drop-ins may not be enough. If your corporate culture has been closed in the past, very few people will have the courage to cross your threshold. Instead, go to the people even though initially it is a much greater time and energy investment.

Southwest Airlines' Herb Kelleher will sit up late at night chatting with a mechanic, and then fix what he hears is wrong. Because an elderly Southwest passenger was worried about changing planes, a Dallas reservations clerk flew with her and helped her through the process. "Employees treat their customers exactly the same way that management treats them."

5. Communicate much more simply and repetitiously than you think is necessary.
Decide on the few main points that need to be made—try to limit them to five or less. The main thrust of a communication should be brief and simple. The same short and clear message needs to be repeated as many times as is necessary.

Never assume the message was received. When a message is sent, find out whether or not anyone heard anything, and if they did, what they believe was said. That lets you know if you need to repeat the message. People are responsible for making sure they've communicated. They have an equal responsibility for being sure they've understood someone else's message. In general, don't ask people directly if they heard the message. If they didn't, they could become defensive. Instead, for example, if a change in policy was communicated, just ask people what they think of the new policy. That way you'll learn if they 'heard.' Then, restate what they said briefly and ask if that was correct. In that way, you'll find out if you 'heard.' Communication must necessarily be a two-way street. And where you assume the communication has been clear because of either physical proximity to another person, or because of close work relationships, those are the areas that should receive the earliest attention at communication correction.

A Chief Operations Officer for a finance company (Peter) asked me to evaluate a chief information officer (Tom) who reported to him. The Information officer had no idea what the COO wanted him to do. I asked Tom to create a list of what he believed were the most important things the COO wanted him to do, and I asked the COO to write down the ten most important things he wanted CIO to accomplish. Both people created reasonable, but uncorrelated, lists. One month later, Peter called to celebrate the changes that he thought I had made. Tom was now accomplishing everything he wanted done. He was so pleased he wanted me to come back and repeat whatever the process was with everyone else.

Communication Guides

Make most communications in person. In-person communications are usually significantly more effective than those by print, video, and electronics. The latter should be viewed as back-up communications, reinforcing the in-person message.

Communicate successes and early wins. Publicize and celebrate people's, team's, and unit's accomplishments. Too often, management doesn't celebrate achievement, share good news, and reveal about the future. If there's good news, publicize it!

Acknowledge difficulties and even failures. The tone of the message can still be positive because even negative experiences can teach how to improve. Speak about hard times because if the topic is avoided and people learn about it, they will be convinced there's a hidden agenda. Hidden agendas preclude trust.

Communicating effectively isn't always a matter of words. In the long run, what's done counts more than what's said. Walk the talk. Do what you say you will do. It's not okay for the leadership to freeze subordinate's wages and give themselves large bonuses when the company isn't making money. It's not walking the talk when the company has diversity programs and everyone with significant power is white and male. One California utility didn't walk the talk when the executives said the organization would focus on customers and then closed their print and graphics unit, which year after year had received the highest ratings in being customer focused.

How to Motivate Others

Everyone's motivated, it's just that people do things
for their reasons not yours. If you want something,
find out what will benefit the other person.
People do things for their reasons, not ours.

A young man and his girlfriend were at a drive in, when the young woman said "Oh, if only we could gaze up at the moon and the stars I would feel so romantic." The top came down. Later, when the young man was bragging about the evening with his friends, he said "It took me only 20 minutes to get that top down!" His friend replied,"Twenty minutes!? it takes me only 10 seconds!" Whereupon the young man shot back proudly, "Yeah, but you've got a convertible." When people want something badly enough, they will move heaven and earth (and car roofs) to get it. Your job is to create the conditions that make it more likely that they want something badly, not to create the desire. That has to come from inside.

Celebrate
Celebrate successes and small, early wins. These celebrations can be as simple as a group lunch, or as complex as some of the following celebrations. Corporations celebrate with branch colors, rap songs, branch cheers, T-shirts. Many cor-

porate meetings are like Mary Kay sales rallies. Nordstrom announces the top twenty salespeople every morning over loudspeakers. At a recent Home Depot opening in Seattle, 150 employees in parking lot form circle, store cheers, turn toward Eagle hardware and yell Who we gonna beat? Eagle! At Kaufman & Broad Home Corp., employees have leapt out of airplanes stopped rush-hour traffic and clothed an elephant. The California home builder gave its 1,200 employees a company T-shirt and challenged them to get the most exposure possible for it. The winner of the 'short-sleeved ad campaign' would get an expense-paid weekend for two in Manhattan. Among the more than 200 entries in the contest was an employee who wore the shirt sky diving, one who persuaded a gondolier in Venice, Italy, to wear it and one who wore the shirt while posing as a mannequin in a Beverly Hills department-store window. Top prize went to 100 employees for slowing 5:00 PM traffic parading in their T-shirts over a freeway overpass in San Francisco. An estimated 30,000 people drove by and saw the shirts.

Reward and reinforce employee behavior that you are trying to increase.

Employees value recognition from their superiors more than many managers realize.

1. Tell them. Praise their efforts immediately; say "good job" or "thank-you." That's all it takes. Congratulate them on as many accomplishments as you can. They will not become complacent, nor will you need to give them more money just because you are praising them.

2. Tell somebody else. Write a letter to your superior, or to the company president, explaining what good work your employee is doing.

3. Show them. Send a card; leave a flower or small gift on the person's desk; take the employee out to lunch.

Set numerical goals to measure results. Goals are important, but they're useful only if you can measure your results accurately. As much as possible, set goals that result in the final behavior. For example, asking your sales staff to make 30 calls an hour, even though related to final sales results, is less effective than simply stating close x bookings at x dollars.

The 'star point' system at Westinghouse assigns each team member responsibility for dealing with internal and external customers. Six months to a year after the team is established, members are graded on performance from customer satisfaction to communication skills, administrative abilities and training curriculum chosen. Each team is cross-trained to fully understand the job functions of other team members on whom they depend. Personal accountability is an integral part of team success, avoiding the 'doubles teams theory'—when balls bounce between partners but neither takes the blame. Cigna's customer service division in Bethlehem, PA has a 'Cheers for Peers' program, recognizing folks for outstanding effort with everything from thank you notes to gift certificates and movie tickets. Special achievements earn a gold leaf, often displayed as a badge of honor in the workplace. It's instant, and it's visual.

Kodak created an 'R-Plus' list, asking each team member what form of reinforcement worked best for them. More often than not, an informal expression of gratitude topped the list. The Team Zebra gang uses a four-part system called 'A Buck's Worth,' whereby supervisors solicited and delivered feedback from management, peers, customers, and the individual on how well each team member met or exceeded expectations. The process reinforced personal achievement, and kept supervisors abreast of each partner's desire for further career development.

Structure rewards in such a way that they are attainable for everyone. The back-pats and thank-you's don't cost a thing. And you don't have to wait for an annual review to say it.

Air Products devised a multi-tiered bonus system ranging from $100 awards for 'above and beyond' daily performance to the annual Chairman's with $50,000 in cash and company stock. Other bonus incentives include a month's pay based on quarterly business unit performance; milestone awards contingent on meeting specific goals; and performance and preferred stock plans based on leadership and individual achievements. Groups are free to develop their own plans based on cost savings, safety and environmental factors.

Pay for Performance can turn workers into rival gangs. At Lantech, a manufacturer of packaging machinery in Louisville, workers tried to stiff a competing division for the toilet paper bill. In 1993, the Conference Board surveyed 382 companies and found that three-quarters provided some form of incentive pay, including bonuses for cost-saving suggestions or for learning new skills.

Many corporations are starting to reward everyone in the company more equally, giving all employees, say, bonuses equivalent to 5% of their salaries, rather than 7% to some employees and 3% to others. At Lantech, each of the company's five manufacturing divisions was given a bonus determined by how much profit it made. An individual worker's share of the bonus could amount to as much as 10% of his or her regular pay. The groups clashed, each one trying to assign costs to the other and claim credit for revenues. were spending 95% of their time on conflict resolution, instead of on how to serve our customers.

Increase employee motivation by increasing participation. Studies show that traditional incentives such as promotions and pay raises aren't the most important factors influencing employee performance. Instead, people tend to work harder for companies which respect them as individuals, take account of their needs and special skills, and include them in actions and decisions affecting their work. Some ways your company can motivate people to do their best work include:

❏ Allow employees to solve problems on their own. Let them know that you have confidence in their judgment and their ability to make decisions.

❏ Encourage teamwork. Let groups work together to make decisions. Their cooperation will spill over into other areas.

❏ Provide information. Information is crucial during a crisis, and just as important when sailing is smooth. Lack of information leads to apathy or a wait-and-see attitude.

❏ Be flexible. When job demands are too rigid, many employees lose their motivation and interest in doing good work. Try to take individual needs into account when considering rules and policies.

❏ Encourage variety and growth. Give employees the chance to learn new skills or work in different areas. The knowledge gained may help people look at old situations in a new light.

❏ Encourage efforts with self-reviews. A Menlo Park personnel services survey showed that 72% believe employee self-ratings 'encourages employee awareness of strengths and weaknesses,' and 59% say it 'aids in gaining commitment to performance goals.' Only 13% of the companies in the survey had such a system set up.

Look back over the notes you've made in the margins in this chapter. Condense them into two action points; two changes you will make as a result of reading this section.

Actions to take:

1._____

2._____

Chapter Twelve
Managing in the InfoWorld

Technology can make you a loser,
but it can't make you a winner.

What are the current technological changes, may be less salient for our purposes than information about how to manage information and manage people through technological change. Many folks think automating will be the magic bullet to save their company.

A motorist was traveling up Highway 99 toward Visalia, California when a three-legged chicken zoomed past him on the dirt shoulder. He raced to catch up, and saw the chicken take a fast right into a farmhouse and disappear around the back of a large building in the rear of the house. He knocked on the door of the house, gasping and excited, "You can't believe what I saw run behind your house. Must have been going 80-90 mph, a chicken with three legs. The farmer acknowledged the chicken. "Oh yeah I know about them, we genetically altered a hen a few generations back to produce a chicken with three legs. My wife and son and myself all fight over drumsticks and producing a chicken with three legs just made sense at the time." Sensing enormous financial potential, the traveller asked how they tasted. The farmer replied: "Don't know yet, they goes so fast we ain't caught one yet."

Technology changes are only as good as the ones you can use and incorporate into your system and the ones that help you improve your business. Don't automate for the sake of automation and never automate a chaotic system. If a disorganized system is automated, you just get more and faster disorganization.

If you automate chaos, you get more chaos.

Telecommuting
In 1950, people bought cars to get to work. Now people are buy computers to work from anywhere. Since Hewlett-Packard's pilot programs started in 1990, more than 2,500 HP employees telecommute at least one day a week. Telecommuting is growing at a rate of 20% a year. A 1996 Bell Atlantic study estimates that over two million businesses have telecommuting policies, up from 1.3 million in 1995. Aetna Life Insurance, Levi Strauss, Hewlett-Packard, Motorola, Pacific Bell, IBM, American Express, Ernst and Young, AT&T, Compaq, Nortel, 3-Com, DEC, MCI, Intel, United Airlines, Apple, Texas Instruments and Du Pont all telecommute. The U.S. federal government plans to have about 3% of the federal workforce telecommuting by the end of 1998, savings of $150 million annually. As of early 1996, over nine million Americans telecommute to work and 14.2 million others operate small businesses from their homes. Because of telecommuting, work is no longer a destination, but a function.

Link Resources, a New York-based research house, estimates that the number of telecommuters will increase from 5.5 million in 1991 to more than 10 million by 1998. The

Department of Transportation predicts that over 15% of the U.S. work force will be telecommuting by 2002.

Marketing reps in Xerox's virtual sales office program 'Work from Anywhere' download up-to-date product and pricing data from corporate databases, transmit new sales orders electronically and check on inventory and the delivery status of pending orders. When Xerox's work force transformation is complete, up to 4,000 sales and marketing reps will no longer need office space.

Teleconferencing centers, already saving millions of travel dollars for giants such as Hewlett-Packard and IBM, are spreading to all sizes of company. One study showed that employees who teleconference learn at the same level in half the time and at half the cost. Hewlett-Packard showed that a 120-site network in the United States, Europe and Canada paid for itself in eight days due to travel savings. Most video-conferencing has massively redundant backup systems to prevent failure.

Telecommuting technologies will reinforce and accelerate the movement of people and enterprises from the center to the periphery. More people will live in edge cities and in small-town and rural America, connected to their workplaces or their markets electronically. Distributed work will result in decreased demand for downtown office space. Virtual organizations link people in scattered locations around shared missions and common tasks. Work will soon move electronically to different time zones every eight hours, providing customer access on a 24-hour basis.

The pressures of global competition, the need for 24-hour customer support, improvements in technology, the need to meet employee flexibility as well as cut overhead has produced a virtual world. Jack Nines in *Making Telecommuting Happen* estimates that a person working at home two days a week, saves a company $12,000 a year as a result of increased productivity, reduced office space and lower turnover. For example, The Dallas Museum of Art hired Dorothy Kosinski as curator even though she lives in Basel, Switzerland. Long-distance relationships also avoid the cost of relocation, often about $80,000 per employee. Telecommuting allows organizations to employ physically challenged people, parents with young children and members of dual career families.

Electronic Partnering
The production schedule at Toyota was 60 days only a few years ago: today, it's three days. Hino Motors, a Japanese truck manufacturer, can now produce over 1,900 different types of trucks with a lead time of under five days. At Toyota, when a dealer places an order for a specific vehicle, the order goes directly into Toyota's production schedule. Toyota does not then place orders for the required parts, because its suppliers automatically check the production schedule and deliver the required mix and quantity as needed. In turn, the suppliers do not bill Toyota for their deliveries. Toyota reviews its production schedule to determine the amount it owes each supplier. Order entry, fulfillment, and payment not only occur with minimal delay, but with minimal over head. Toyota experiences big reductions in traditional overhead functions and costs.

To design, produce, deliver, and also finance products requires that all links in the business chain be tied very closely together. Although suppliers, manufacturers, distributors, and retailers may still exist as independent companies, the interdependencies among them are now so total that the concept of an arm's-length relationship is disappearing completely.

Multiple suppliers used to be the rule, and automakers often played suppliers off against each other for price and other concessions. Those old relationships are being displaced by new electronic relationships. The network that links General Motors to its suppliers and dealers is changing how it operates more dramatically than it is changing what it produces. This means embracing a world of customer self design, mass customization, rapid response, on-demand manufacture, zero inventory, and closely-coupled relationships that are held together electronically.

Networking
The set of relationships you create and maintain with suppliers, allies, distributors, and customers, to manufacture and market your product may be your most important business strategy of the future. Buyers seek out suppliers who do offer electronic linkages, or who have accessible information systems. Pen Notes Inc., a $1.3-million designer and manufacturer was told by J.C. Penney to go on-line for ordering and invoicing. The Cedar Works Inc., in Peebles, Ohio, got pushed on-line by Wal-Mart. Today, Cedar Works is an $18-million company, on-line with 10 major retailers, including Home Depot Inc., Target Stores, and Nature Co. Inc.

In the past, if you built a mouse trap, the world beat a path to your door. Today, the game is to build a better path. Whoever owns the information pathways will call the shots. Electronic integration is clustering firms with common electronic pathways. The Japanese call these clusters keiretsu groups. Mitsubishi, the largest keiretsu group, is a circle of twenty-eight companies surrounded by thousands of other manufacturers, suppliers, distributors, and affiliates.

The Virtual Company
VeriFone, a credit card-verification company founded in 1982, was a virtual company from the beginning. Every time you hand a credit card to a clerk or waiter, you probably do business with Verifone, who makes card-swipe terminals and controls 60% of the United States market for authorization services. They now have a portable wireless version for vendors such as taxi drivers and pizza stand operators. The company has no secretaries, no internal paper mail, and all communication is via Internet. When a Verifone employee

encounters a tough customer negotiation, he can leave the negotiation, send in requests to headquarters, and get instant guidance.

But they've faced the same problems that existing businesses face when they try to introduce innovations: the difficulty of changing deeply entrenched workplace habits. **Here are eight steps they have taken to create a virtual company:**

1. Automate tasks that waste people's time. Start by automating those processes that are most time-consuming or prone to error. Don't enter data twice. At VeriFone they use more than 60 different computer-based applications. All aspects of corporate life mean interaction with an on-line system.

2. Create a company-wide electronic filing cabinet. When a company's reports and forms, as well as its E-mail correspondence, are filed on-line, the on-line system becomes a global electronic filing cabinet. All that you need to access contracts, approvals, and old correspondence is a computer and a telephone line. If I'm in a hotel room in one part of the world and it's two in the morning at my corporate headquarters in San Diego, I can still pull up a contract and make changes so that my people have the revision when they get to work the next morning. Too much time is wasted at most companies because employees can't put their hands on the right document when they need it.

3. People *must* go on-line. You can't just make the technology available and wait for your company to convert itself into a virtual one. Give people a reason to use the tools. Take away the alternatives. Begin by abolishing written memos and insisting that messages be sent on-line with a back-up only when policy has changed. Put news items that are relevant to your business and your customers on-line. Most sites use auto-responders to pass information without human intervention. If your employees know they can get information that will help them in their jobs, they'll go on-line to find it.

4. Make systems easy to use. Otherwise bright people can freeze when faced with a bunch of arcane commands. The more you put on-line, the more important it is to make them friendly. Make every report or information template accessible from a single Menu command, from which one may navigate through simple hierarchical option lists.

5. Train in responsible communication. Certain messages are best reserved for face-to-face communication. Responsible communication means considering how a recipient is likely to react to a message, and what the implications are for the recipients workload. Confrontation is easier by E-mail than face to face, but can create resentment that is destructive.

How to Convert to a Virtual Office
1. Provide adequate computer equipment, hookups and support services to those at home, either through direct purchase, lease or employee cost-share. The Shepp's in *The Telecommuter's Handbook* (McGraw-Hill, 1995), surveyed 100 telecommuting companies and found that 48% supplied all the necessary equipment for telecommuters. Another 26% shared the equipment expense with their telecommuters. Pacific Bell budgeted $4,000 a person a year for home office needs; Hewlett-Packard's spending ranged from $4,000 to $6,000. According to Gil Gordon, in the July 1994 *Telecommuting Review*, the payback period for the technology investment to set up a virtual office ranges from six to twelve months.

2. Partially substitute for social and professional isolation. Grantham found that virtual office workers spend 43% of their time interacting with other workers. Sixty-one percent reported that they contacted their co-workers two or more times per day and 94% of the virtual workforce check in three or more times a week. Schedule monthly meetings for all employees to compare notes and socialize. Carry a pager, a cellular phone and a laptop and check voice mail. Most employees who report are similarly equipped. And all have copies of each other's electronic schedules.

3. Make sure the employee has suitable work space and a domestic situation to be productive.

4. Help employees manage the work-home blur. Some telecommuters can't control the 'off' switch. (Give guidelines). As companies downsize, more and more work is heaped on fewer and fewer workers. Workaholics have trouble ending their day; many report ten to twelve-hour days.

5. Absorb the telecommuter's cost of doing business. It's a small price to pay considering the saving in overhead.

6. Learn a management style suitable for the future. Command-and-control management cannot work even when employees are in the office. Remote managers need excellent communications skills, a work style with high trust between employee and manager, and managing by results.

Guidelines
With hoteling, employees work at home. They keep an office open as a management control center, with administrative support and empty 'hotel offices.' Remember that business used to be transacted at the coffee machine, the watercooler or the impromptu departmental lunch. Isolating workers in their homes not only diminishes their social life, but cuts out a critical aspect of corporate culture that leads to a dynamic business. Much important communication takes place informally. The use of video conferencing, virtual meeting spaces and groupware should help.

Perkin-Elmer, makers of scientific and lab equipment, reduced more than 50 sales offices to seven, gave each sales and service engineer a furniture allowance of $1,000, a fax machine, a 486 laptop with modem, and two phone lines for their home offices.

Advantages

Sick time is down. People work longer hours and with more workdays than average with two less sick days per year. Companies can keep going even if the offices are destroyed. Telecommuting companies got back in business within hours of the San Francisco and Northridge earthquakes. Federal employees in Oklahoma City worked in satellite telework centers located in the suburbs. Workers share offices, using them on alternate days. IBM shrunk 400,000 feet of office space into a 100,000 designed on the "hotel" principle: Workers check in with a computerized secretary that assigns them a cubicle and switches their calls to the appropriate cubby.

Texas-based telework consultant Joanne Pratt found, when surveying over 17,000 telecommuters, that remote workers receive promotions at a greater rate than nontelecommuters.

Rent in cyberspace is cheaper than catalogue space, and much lower than mall rent. There are 12 million miles of optical fiber in the U.S. and the greatest purchasers of fiber-optical cable is the electric utility industry.

The race is going to be won by those people who have guts and are willing to spend the money now.

You don't always have to be first in everything to gain dominance. The leading edge of an aircraft wing just collects bugs and ice; the real lift is about one-third of the way back. So, as long as you're in the front half of a trend, you don't need to be first.

It's like the land rush in Oklahoma. The best spot in the valley goes to the one who gets there first. Being first also has the highest death rate.
Larry Ellison, of Oracle

Don't look at automating what you're doing.
Look at why you're doing it and whether you should
do it at all. Only then, look at the technology.
Jim Grant

Implementing a new Information System? Companies who've been successful have answered these questions first:

1. Did employees give their opinions about the proposed technology change before the project received the official go-ahead?

2. Do employees perceive that the change will benefit them?

3. Have the employees who will be using the new technology taken part in early testing? Were employee suggestions used?

4. Do you have a formal training strategy for bringing workers up to speed?

5. Do you have core people trained in the new technology who can act as resources?

You can have the best system in the world,
but if you can't pay for it because your business is off,
what's the use of having it?

 Look back over the notes you've made in the margins in this chapter. Condense them into two action points; two changes you will make as a result of reading this section.

Actions to take:

1._____

2._____

Chapter Thirteen
Reactions to Change

You can't stop the waves,
but you can learn how to surf.
Zen saying

Corruption begins when people start saying one thing,
and thinking another.
Vaclav Havel

When people become aware of change through the grapevine, information is tripled in amplitude and scope. Like all other animals, people stop what they are doing, sit up, and take notice. If rumors increase, usually distorted, fear begins. Anger, hostility and feelings of betrayal can ensue quickly if there is no formal company communication.

Our companies are filled with extreme anxiety. People are intimidated, sometimes by autocratic and demeaning supervision, but more often by a system that is directionless and seems out of control. Whatever the cause, people will not 'embrace change,' unless the atmosphere in the organization is supportive and encouraging.

Whenever we're asked to change, the first instinctual response is "what am I going to lose?" If this natural response isn't managed in a company, mass paranoia begins.

People isolate themselves and compete with one another. We tend to communicate less when we need to communicate even more. Jane Goodall's studies of chimps at the Gombe Stream Reserve in Africa showed that when normally good-natured chimps living in a lush jungle with lots of dinner for everyone, were given what they perceived to be a limited source of food, they started grabbing bananas from other chimps, hoarding, and taking off with them. The dominant chimps wouldn't share, and the submissive ones had to beg for scraps.

> *Division is the best sign for the enemy.*
> *When you are divided and competing,*
> *you become the next meal for outside sources.*

Allow for Losses. Whether real or perceived, losses always result in feeling cut off, even if the loss is simply a loss of familiar methods and procedures (Bridges, 1994). People tend to exaggerate losses to cope with them, and if they have no former experience with the current losses, the experience can be especially unsettling. Lingering worry, anger, resentment, confusion, even passive-aggressive or antisocial behavior are all typical responses.

> *Take what is good from the past.*
> *There are no maps, just compasses.*
> *Make links between the old and new to clarify a direction*
> *and goal so people have something to hang onto.*

If you jump to new beginnings too quickly, you may forget the necessity of transition and ending time. Allow time for reflection and understanding of reactions to change. The emotions accompanying transitions are difficult and unwieldy. When loss occurs, people may go through unpredictable and difficult stages of shock or denial, anger, confusion, and depression before acceptance. Move through whatever stages are necessary.

Examining your own personal endings may help you to understand employees' reactions. Think back to a time when something *you* enjoyed had to end–whether a job, relationship, or party. Before you *knew* it was going to end, how did it feel? How were you getting along with others? What made it end? How did you react initially? After awhile, you had a different response, what was it? How did it turn out–how are things now? This is the complex process others are experiencing right now.

Response #1 Hiding

Denial is effective to help us work through passages that otherwise would be too painful. Animals go into shock states when they are near death, for example. Losses can trigger denial where the level of self-esteem is so low that there are no resources or reserves left. Loss of security, a feeling of competence, having to perform new, unfamiliar tasks without skills, loss of a sense of belonging, loss of a sense of direction, loss of control over space–can all trigger denial.

> *A man has no ears for that to which*
> *experience has given him no access.*
> Nietzsche

Under rapid or dramatic change, people start working harder, reorganize, cut costs and downsize, *so they can keep things the way they were.* Suffering a loss of market share, they may get facelifts, start blaming, panic, go back to basics, and continue in denial. One of the clearest signs of shock is that the company does even more of what they were doing before trauma. Following a 1994 California earthquake, the rescue team found people amidst the rubble, cleaning kitchen counter tops, or tidying up workbenches, as if nothing had happened. They may have acknowledged a rumble around them, but were oblivious to the mass destruction and to the possibility that their friends and neighbors were fatally wounded and their homes destroyed.

> *Given a choice between changing and proving that it is not*
> *necessary, most people get busy on the proof.*
> John Galbraith, Economist

There was little to be done for those in denial, or in 'hiding,' other than to provide basic sustenance and protection from further trauma. Their ability to respond appropriately was impaired, and psychologically they were fragile. The belief system which was protecting them from acknowledging the extent of the trauma was the same system that was preventing them from adapting.

Organizations in shock, like individuals, not only hang on to old ways, they will hang on to employees who have ceased productivity way beyond the time they should be released. If you are a manager, how many times have you put extra effort into an employee that you knew, deep down, wasn't right? When something in the environment is not understandable to us, and we have no current methods for understanding it, we tend to perseverate or to fix on the object until, we assume, we will be able to master it. Victims of post-traumatic stress experience a type of fixation or perseveration. The event or image may mentally continue to recur until it becomes understandable. Only then can the mental system release it.

Don't wait until denial teaches you or your company, life's difficult '2 x 4' experiences, or those times when you have to be struck on the head with a 2x4 board in order to get it. A multi-billion dollar Midwestern food company dismissed the need for succession planning until after one of its corporate jets crashed, killing several top executives. A 50-year-old woman refused to quit her three-pack-a-day habit until she was diagnosed with lung cancer and had one lung removed. An electric utility ignored the need for a formal policy against sexual harassment until after it was faced with expensive lawsuits. An electronics giant scoffed at attempts of a new competitor to enter their market. American auto makers denied the need to retool until Japan took over and captured much of the market. Ongoing denial of economic realities resulted in dramatic upheaval in the Soviet Union.

> *Someone who redoubles his efforts*
> *when he's forgotten his aim.*
> Santayana's definition of a fanatic.

For companies in Stage One, I recommend:

1. People in denial need to stay in denial until their fear subsides and further information allows them to develop insight. You cannot coach, bribe, threaten, cajole or force people or companies out of denial. Let them be.

> *As Louis Armstrong said about jazz:*
> *If you can't feel it, I can't define it.*

2. Even though you cannot change people in denial, their denial prevents them from protecting themselves. Consequently, you may need to remove people in denial from danger and provide protection. Their delusional state prevents them from interpreting and acting on reality appropriately. If you are employing these people, you may need to, as we say here in California, 'release them to the universe,' if they refuse to accept reality. You are not doing them a favor by by letting them hang on to their denial. Sometimes it's healthiest to be blunt:

> *Cuando el caballo esta muerto, dejalo.*
> 'When your horse is dead, get off it.'

3. Don't feed into their denial by pretending to go along with their unrealistic statements and beliefs. Simply state how you feel and think.

People are in denial because they don't know any differently. Educate and expose them, but recognize that they are not strong enough to change. Validating them, and increasing their self-esteem can work indirectly. Set these people up for small wins, limited projects related to the future over which they *can* have some control. That might form as a link over the bridge of fear. Recognize and rescue the 'obsolete' employee, or those who dwell on the past and resist change. The danger signs of 'worker obsolescence' include lack of initiative; exclusive focus on the day-to-day; waning enthusiasm; and growing defensiveness.

Think of self-esteem as a jar of jelly beans. Change requires giving up beans. If they don't have enough for survival, they will refuse, usually at the unconscious and survival level. Or, think of change requiring a tremendous burst of energy, flooring the accelerator in your car. If there's not enough gas, they know best to just cruise along. However, just as the folks in the movie Jurassic Park couldn't hide from the dinosaurs, people in denial can't hide forever. The future will find them.

> *Don't try to change people.*
> *Technology will obsolete them.*
> Buckminster Fuller

Stage Two: Stuck

Many of the earthquake population in California were wandering around dazed, confused, frightened and in panic. One could work with these people because there was some access to their psychological system. They were out of denial and acknowledged the severity of the damage and the peril they were still in, but because of their own emotional needs, they weren't able to help either themselves or others. However, they did listen enough to be able to prepare for further trauma. People in Stage Two needed clear, simple directions to protect from themselves and constant reassurance. There was nothing that could "calm them down" and in fact, it wasn't one of the rescuers' goals. They were working through the disaster in the way they could, and their reaction would eventually repair itself. The only limitation was on panic/hysteria; just as in workplace negativity, it becomes infectious and can disturb a whole unit.

Because people and companies in Stage Two acknowledge the problem, but still don't have the resources with which to deal with it, they place responsibility outside themselves. Thus, they tend to whine about problems incessantly. Even though it seems to provide them with some temporary relief, everybody around them gets sick. Typhoid Mary was a waitress at the turn of the century in New York City who was a typhoid carrier. She experienced no symptoms, but she passed Typhoid to everyone who she served.

Hearing others complain incessantly is much like living around emotional second hand smoke. It's just as toxic to your emotional system as smoke is to your physical system. Complaining never solves anything, it just makes it worse. If everyone joined hands to form a human circle, looked up to the sky and complained in unison about the tough business environment, would it change anything? Now, by complaining I don't mean the open and honest statement of our difficulties, challenges, and expression of depression and other emotive states. I mean using complaining as a method of avoiding action. Although we used to think that continual voicing of the negative would provide relief, it seems that being continually negative and complaining is a form of Obsessive-Compulsive Disorder (OCD), wherein the negative thoughts and voiced complaints become ruminative in nature. The best form of treatment is not to indulge them, but to stop them.

Signs that a company is in Stage Two:
Rumors, secret meetings, tension and chaos, accident health care claims and absences, complaining, passivity, blaming. For companies and people in Stage Two, I recommend:

1. Clear, but limited forums for employees to voice their concerns.
2. Good training in communication and conflict resolution skills.
3. Guidelines to help those who work with negative people.

We're going on a journey. We're going
to carry our wounded, and shoot our dissenters.
Bob Allen, CEO, AT&T

At least, people in Stage Two are progressing from denial toward acceptance. Resistance is a positive sign, because attitudes are beginning to change. For example, if you grew up in a severely dysfunctional family, everything probably seemed 'fine' until certain age, because you were in denial. Because you didn't have the development to understand, you were protected from understanding. You realized your parents were disturbed only when you had the ability to react against it, or when you were capable of surviving on your own. Many people are still in denial; that is, they continue to view their childhoods as 'normal' even though they are experiencing chronic problems with relationships and emotional expression. One needs to acknowledge the truth before being able to move past it.

Stage Three: Getting on Board
Stage Three, or the beginning acceptance stage, indicates that things are ready to move, and people are beginning to begin to establish priorities. It's an exciting phase for any individual, full of new ideas, and different approaches. In this stage, put employees in charge of change by letting them make decisions and carry out assignments. Form transition teams to give people a vested interest in success of change. This is the stage of cooperation, an ability to strive toward excellence, where it was difficult before this stage. Keep monitoring change however, because there will be relapses. Many companies fall into old routines because there was no follow up and review when departments and employees reach stage three. Autocratic management and orders at this stage, and avoidance and silence can destroy or prevent focused change.

The old, predictable stages of change no longer apply; the world is too complex. In understanding change reactions, know that Stages One, Two, and Three are uneven, and do not progress in a linear way. Thus, expect that you, and your organization, will flip-flop back and forth among the stages. As long as you are moving in the direction of your vision, and your truth, you are doing the right thing.

 Look back over the notes you've made in the margins in this chapter. Condense them into two action points; two changes you will make as a result of reading this section.

Actions to take:

1._____

2._____

Chapter Fourteen
Change Resistance

The biggest single challenge has been, and will continue to be, to change people's habits.
John F. Akers, former IBM Chairman

Resistance is a healthy sign. It beats apathy.

Why do People Resist?
Definitions and theories abound in the psychological literature in the 20th century, discussing advanced defensive systems such as repression, transference, and secondary gain. As theoretically intriguing these may be, they hardly profit the manager who is responsible for others, the determined person in the throes of finally trying to change herself, or the parent trying to overcome resistance that has built up in her children.

The dictionary defines resistance as: *an act or instance of resisting. 2. the ability to resist; esp. the inherent capacity of a living being to resist untoward circumstances as disease, malnutrition, or toxic agents. 3. an opposing or retarding force 4a. the opposition offered by a body or substance to the passage through it of a steady electric current b: a source of resistance.*

More simply stated, then, resistance is what people are doing when they do what you don't want them to do. Given that people are not doing what you would like them to do, it may be important to make basic distinctions.

Very occasionally, and this may shock the reader, others may have a perfectly sound reason for doing what they are doing, and to *not* resist you would be dysfunctional. Thus, you may have no right to impose your will on others. At other times, it may be necessary for a company or group to change for everyone's benefit, that a critical mass be on board and moving in the same direction. It becomes critical then, that the manager have the skills of learning to recognize resistance, understand for what it is, develop a healthy reaction to it, and behave in a way that is most likely to reduce it. This chapter (s) will help do that.

First, let's understand some basics:

Resistance is healthy
Just as electrical conductance is slowed by resistance, resistance to an idea can provide the whole system with more time to consider the change. Approached from this perspective, resistance can be welcomed as a natural safeguard. People can resist change, then, when it is unhealthy to comply. Resistance is an expected and normal part of the human condition.

Why People Change
We are born with a willingness to change; it's adaptive to do so. Although change is not generally resisted, people do change only under exceptional circumstances:

People change:

❑ when the pain is so great that continuing in the present state would be life-threatening. Change here is driven by survival.

❑ to satisfy a deeper need, to prove they can do it, or to challenge or defy others. Included in these are healthy needs such as the need for competence and control over one's environment.

❑ as a way of life and become addicted to change groups, or change cultures such as new age churches, cults, change gurus.

❑ when the fear of changing is less than the pain of staying the same. When the consequences of smoking are just too much greater than the consequences of quitting. When the approach avoidance conflict balance changes.

The Approach-Avoidance Conflict
The *Approach-Approach* conflict arises when there are two equally *attractive* goals. No movement can take place unless and until there is a change in the balance, or weight between these two goals. This can be achieved either mentally or in reality. For example, you cannot decide two equally attractive cars. To break the stalemate, one car's price needs to increase, or a favorable review needs to be published about the other, for the conflict to be resolved. In the *Approach-Avoidance* conflict, the desirability of the goal and the pain of staying the same are equal in energy so there is no movement. Similarly, there is a need to change the attractiveness or unattractiveness of either goal. The *Avoidance-Avoidance* conflict arises when there are two equally *unattractive* goals. No movement can take place unless and until there is a change in the balance, or weight between these two goals. This can be achieved either mentally or in reality. For example, you cannot decide two equally unattractive choices, such as visiting relatives you don't like for Thanksgiving, versus staying home and painting the house.

One factor provoking most resistance is that most people want change to be easy. When they discover it isn't, they interpret the difficulty as terrible, and that they shouldn't have to endure it. They think that others should see how hard it is for them to change, and should give them more help than they are presently, at the least should notice and offer sympathy (Ellis, 1985).

People don't want to be uncomfortable.
The lower the frustration tolerance,
the higher the fundamental opposition to change.

Scott Peck said it succinctly: "Life is difficult. This is a great truth, one of the greatest truths. It is a great truth because once we truly see this truth, we transcend it. Once we truly know that life is difficult—once we truly understand and accept it—then life is no longer difficult. Because once it is accepted, the fact that life is difficult no longer matters." (Peck, 1992).

Everybody wants to go to heaven, but nobody wants to die.
Senator Walter Huddleston D-KY

Frustration Tolerance
One reason why change is difficult for some people is the tendency for immature, or less emotionally developed people, to have a low frustration tolerance. Thus, when things are difficult, things are discarded rather than attempted. The easy way is taken. With a low frustration tolerance, it becomes hard to delay gratification, and yet it is in the delay of immediate gratification that long term and worthwhile change is accomplished. When a company or any unit contains a critical mass of persons who are able to delay immediate gratification for higher or longer term goals, chances are that company will be able to move forward. If, for some reason, most employees demand that their immediate needs and wishes be met, and they are unwilling to deny short-term goals for longer term ones, then that unit or company may derail in its change efforts. These people can be dragged kicking and screaming only by the most resolute and determined of lead-

ers. Sadly, some companies whose leaders themselves have had problems delaying gratification are filled with those like themselves.

Recent literature indicates that one of the major problems of our society is the inability to delay gratification, resulting from overindulgent generation where each whim was granted or that there was insufficient attention to limits and controls so that children did not learn to deal with frustration or delay gratification. Gottfurcht (1995), in fact, lists inability to delay gratification as one of the reasons why both individuals and our countries are so in debt.

Here, it might be helpful to understand the reversing consequence gradient.

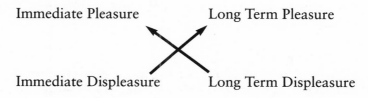

Immediate Pleasure   Long Term Pleasure

Immediate Displeasure   Long Term Displeasure

Your personal solution seems clear:

1. Understand the unforgiving nature of the law of reversing consequence.

2. Discipline yourself to reach longer-term goals. There is no magic bullet. Just as you strengthen your muscular system by constant exercise and weight resistance, so too, will you strengthen your mental muscles. When you have outlined a long-term goal, but become distracted by a shorter term, immediate pleasure goal,try the following statement: "I want this, but if I have it/do it, I will not reach my goal. If I don't reach my long-term goals, the following will result: _____. If I *do* reach my long-term goals, the following will result: _____. Thus, I will wait ten minutes to indulge this short-term goal." Then, repeat every ten min-

utes for as man years as you need to, to reach your long-term goals. I remember repeating the above statement for the eight years of full-time study that it took to receive a doctoral degree, for the six months of active withdrawal from nicotine, and many times for withdrawal from relationships.

The reversing consequent gradient is active in organizations as well. Recall from earlier chapters that internal change programs programs have failed to meet expectations. Managers have become disillusioned, and their corporations have fallen further behind. According to Preston-Smith (1993), change isn't inhibited by inertia. Rather, resistance occurs when poorly designed or implemented programs activate internal forces that work to derail change efforts—rather like a corporate immune system. Below are listed twelve of the most commonly observed change processes that can derail the change effort. You may want to compare your organization with these descriptions:

1. Top Down

Many change programs fail because employees resist a top-down approach, believing that top management doesn't really understand the problem, and they are typically correct. A better approach is for the CEO to repeatedly describe the problem as she or he sees it to employees, before designing the change program. Then—and this is the most important part—the CEO needs to listen carefully for responses. Interested employees then design the change program.

2. Bottom-Up

Lower level managers are sent to training programs, where they learn techniques for accelerating change. Their supervisors expect a simple quick fix, but misjudge the organizational changes needed. Because change momentum is stuck at the front line levels, it goes nowhere and quickly loses momentum.

3. Too Slow
Many companies start change programs with a broad but detailed change effort, epistles, and fanfare, to build support and understanding among employees. This minimizes the risk of failure, because there is nothing to fail at during the long preparation period. The program either fizzles out for lack of long-term enthusiasm, or takes a long time to complete. It is far faster, more effective, and less risky to start with a small program, strive for success with it, then build on the enthusiasm it generates and the lessons learned.

4. Too Fast
The organization needs time to absorb the impact of change, to alter beliefs and practices, to internalize new concepts, and to synthesize the various new procedures. Just as massed (intense, non-spaced) practice in learning leads to an initially high response rate, it leads to fast forgetting as well. Spaced trials, leaving time between learning episodes, results in a slower acquisition time, but resulting memory is far superior.

5. Wrong Focus
Some companies begin change without first understanding what needs changing, what their strengths are, and where they have failed in similar efforts in the past. One client in a major utility rushed into a project without first understanding the dynamics of the interdepartmental team it was putting together. Because of arguments between the new team leader and a senior engineer, the utility decided to terminate the engineer. This not only was not the problem, it cost it a valuable employee and undermined the organizational change program.

6. Wrong Training
For people to operate in new ways, they often need training in the new skills involved. Some companies recognize this and train people on a widespread basis in anticipation of their new responsibilities. However, because the training is done in a concentrated time period, it is perishable. When people are

thrust into their new roles a few months later, they have for-
gotten what they learned.

Knowledge is more perishable than fresh fish.
Alfred Whitehead

More important, because the training did not seem applicable
or useful to participants when they took the course, they
lacked interest in learning the new skills. Offer training just
before it will be needed, or after a person has had a chance to
struggle in the new role. But do give the training. Among
other benefits, it signals management's support for the
changes the employee is making. Many companies are with-
holding training not only because of costs, but because the
perception of temporal employees.Why should I train my
employees? As soon as I have trained them they leave. One of
the current responsibilities of employers is to train employees
in skills that are applicable long-term.

*There is only one thing worse than training employees and
have them leave, not training them and keeping them.*

7. Spray-gunning
Corporate change programs, especially quality programs, are
usually based on the assumption that each person can change
as easily as any other. Yet, there's a broad spectrum of readi-
ness. Some people are ready for change and will try a new
approach, some will follow the leaders, and some will switch
over only when they see that their career will end if they
don't. Identify the easy converts and start with them, then
work with the middle group, letting the tide of change influence the holdouts.

When corporate change programs involve employee empowerment, which encourages employees to make many of the
decisions formerly made by their bosses but are given neither
the information nor the tools nor the autonomy to make the
decisions, change is resisted. Mid-managers begin to wonder

where they fit in. A major part of any empowerment program must be to redesign and reeducate.

8. Unclear Direction

When working with a company to accelerate common-sense change, one of my first tasks is to query each senior manager as to why the company needs to change and the direction it needs to go. I tend to get a broad variety of answers from the higher levels, with a paradoxical reaction as I work down through the ranks. Although the overall direction becomes more and more unclear, the impact of reality becomes more and more focused. That is, upper echelons are so far out of touch that they tend to cite global changes without clear understanding of how these will be accomplished. The front line knows what changes their company needs to make, but in attributing direction to upper level are not able to lead or even suggest the how's, Everyone knows what to do, nobody will speak up about how to do it.

9. Inconsistent Rewards

When the reward system is consistent with the desired change, all animals work toward the goal. When the reward changes in an erratic fashion, or the animal is punished, or when there is no reward, the brighter animal goes on to greener goal boxes. So, if teamwork is valued over individual contribution, there should be team rewards. If rewards remain unaligned for long, employees will revert to doing what they are paid for. For instance, a company well known for its innovation, has developed a strong dual-ladder system in which technical and managerial employees have equal advancement potential. But now, the company is emphasizing self-managing teams, so it will have to consider a third ladder for team leaders if it expects talented people to leave the established ladders to lead teams.

10. Techno-Change

Sometimes companies try to buy their way through organizational change by in vesting in the latest technology. Often, this amounts to automating a poor way of doing business, further entrenching and sanctioning it. Revise the management process first, then think about possible technological enhancements.

11. Moving Boxes
The time-honored solution to organizational problems is to move the boxes around. If management finds that engineering and manufacturing are not communicating, it reorganizes so that they report to one manager. Then, when it becomes obvious that marketing is left out, the chart is modified some more. These changes on paper seldom affect the way that people actually interact. Analyze how information and material should flow through the organization, then rearrange things to facilitate these flows; for example, have people from different functions actually sitting side by side.

12. Failing to Reinforce
Companies treat successful change efforts as though they were business-as-usual accomplishments, letting successes slip by unmentioned. Watch for even small signs of success or positive changes in behavior, and celebrate these with your employees. This encourages further improvement. Even if the changes are not exactly what is desired, let people know when their be havior is changing in the right direction.

Effecting organizational change is a difficult and demanding process, and even the best-designed programs encounter resistance. However, corporate immunity to change should be viewed as a positive sign of the company's health: Resistance requires energy, and shows that employees are not merely apathetic to management's goals.

Why do people resist?
❑ Fear losing job status business contacts or favorable working conditions
❑ Don't see a need for change
❑ Don't respect the person or department introducing change

❏ Don't like the way change was introduced
❏ Weren't consulted or personally informed about the change
❏ Don't understand the reasons for the change or feel it will do
more harm than good
❏ Consider the change a personal criticism
❏ Think that the change requires too much effort or comes
at a bad time.
❏ Think that the change creates more responsibility and hard work
❏ Want to test the organization to see if they can avoid
implementing the change
❏ Have negative feelings about the organization or their jobs
❏ Have been negatively influenced by their peers or the leaders of
their peer groups.

People accept change when:
❏ They expect more favorable working conditions or an increase in
income, status, authority, and business contacts
❏ Expect more opportunities for growth, recognition, and
promotion
❏ Think the change is needed and the timing right
❏ Like or respect the person or department that introduced the
change
❏ Like the way the change was introduced
❏ Contributed input to the change
❏ Have positive feelings about the organization or their jobs

Five Reasons Why People Won't Change

Convince them that no matter how hard it is for them to change it will be harder for them not to change.

Use natural hedonistic tendencies to reinforce themselves for progress and punish themselves when they don't change.

1. Fear of Disclosure
Fear of opening up, admitting, breaking old taboos. Uncover old taboos for them and help them rethink validity of them. Need to uncover these before they can move on.

2. Hopelessness

It's no use; it's hopeless and I can't change. Go along initially but as soon as something goes wrong, they fall off. Their falling off proves hat it's hopeless and they give up. Giving up proves that they were right. They feel that they should have made it but they didn't, and since they didn't do what they had to, it's terrible. Then they blame themselves for acting like that. Secondary disturbance disturbed about being disturbed .

3. Fear of Change or Fear of Success

There is a need for safety and certainty, and even though their symptoms are uncomfortable, at least they're familiar. If they give up these familiar feelings they may get stuck with something even worse, or nothing at all. They protect against failure, why is public speaking is the greatest fear. As long as I fear it, I excuse myself from doing it, and exposing myself to failure. I can't I have a phobia, as if there's a something out there that's stopping me, when all the time it's me but I can't face that. Fear of failure is usually a fear of subsequent failure.

If I succeed then: I'll lose the indulgence of my friends and family who presently pity me, people will be jealous of me, if this time I'm successful, later on I'll fail at something larger than this. I can do this but it will lead to something bigger then I'll really fall on my face.I'll need to become more responsible and put out too much effort.

4. Reactance

Change is an impingement on freedom, people will fight if even if they asked for the change. The need to control destiny. The old belief persists that 'I can't be directed by anyone else, I won't be led by the nose, I should have perfect control.' Use humor, which creates flexibility, and paradoxical intention. Create a failure to show that it's not terrible and then teach new and more appropriate responses to it.

5. Payoffs

Payoffs are too great from what they are presently doing. If a worker develops coronary symptoms and needs time off, he will not want to give up the symptoms.Discover hidden penalties that will emerge when they change and work with these hidden penalties in advance. For example, a young woman will not lose weight if she is not prepared to deal with the advances young men will make toward her if she does. An engineer cannot develop marketing skills until he also learns to overcome the fear of uncertainty, loss and failure, all components of sales.Identify, dispute, and surrender unhealthy maladaptive goals for adaptive ones.

Resistance is
1.   Often automatic, unconscious.
2.   Held tightly
3.   Accompanied by strong habits.
4.   Hard to change
5.   Likely to re-occur when stressed

Most important, resistance is common, and 'normal.' Children resist parents, students resist teachers, employees resist employers, prospects resist salespeople, marriage partners resist each other. Cognitive Dissonance lies at the basis of most resistance. It's impossible to hold incompatible beliefs and actions. To change your beliefs, I must also change your actions. To change your actions, I must also change your beliefs. It's easier to change actions than beliefs. Beliefs are the foundations, behaviors are the walls.

Below are listed natural resistances of our species:
1. Territorial resistance or 'what's mine is mine' resistance Every animal will protect it territory, whether dogs flowers, trees, or humans.

2. People who look (act, walk, talk) differently than we do. You're overbearing, you make me feel unimportant, your hair is too long, you wear too much makeup, you have curly black

hair and I had an algebra teacher with curly black hair I hated.

3. Personal threats. People who get in too far, or who are too personal, are manipulative, or dishonest, commanding, or demanding.

4. Fear. We fear what we don't understand. A patient can hear the word electrodes and conclude extreme torture, and thus will resist the EEG. Instead of saying "I don't understand," most people will resist.

Manipulations

Manipulations are given in response to requests or demands that exceed one's capacity to deliver. The organism will develop a strategy to distract the requester, so as to avoid responsibility for action. The following are common manipulations:

1. "Give me more detail." A huge amount of time is spent gathering details, and not much time spent deciding what to do. When you begin to get impatient with added questions, it is a good sign of resistance.

2. Floods you with detail. This person will send tons of information, with loads of detail. When you start to get overwhelmed and start to lose focus, it is resistance.

3. Too Busy. "I'd like to go ahead, but the timing is bad. I'm just too busy. I want you to think I'm refusing because of lack of time, not because I feel very uncomfortable with your proposal." "I don't want you to think I don't want to visit my frail and ailing mother, so I am too busy with all my volunteer committees."

4. It's Impractical. "This is the real world. That won't work in the real world. Not practical.

5. Confusion.

6. Silence. "No problem." "If there's a problem I'll tell you." Silence is an extremely aggressive style. If there are few signs of life, you're being resisted.

7. Intellectualizing. The resister will offer complex theories about why things are the way they are. When this theorizing begins at a high tension time or during a tense meeting, it is often resistance.

8. Compliance. This person totally agrees and wants to know what to do next. She wants to get to solutions quickly without discussing the problem.

> *No matter what your manipulator says, recognize that he or she is functioning at the highest level possible at that moment, and is trying to get his or her needs met.*

> *The method by which they are trying is not appropriate, however, and you will be neutralizing a situation by not responding to it.*

If you value the relationship and want to improve communication, you may want to get beyond the manipulation instead if just cutting it off. If someone is using anger with you, ask what it is about your behavior that is so upsetting. The question forces the other person to clarify the personal, subjective basis for the criticism. This makes open discussion possible.

A healthy response is to stop what you are doing as a response to manipulation. If you are unable to change your behavior, do not punish yourself, or fall into the victim role, which may cause you to resent the people who 'hold you back' or 'make you do things.'

> *Manipulators go for easy prey.*
> *You are manipulated only if you let yourself to be.*

The following can be manipulations:
- Being sick or developing physical symptoms
- Being extremely hard working or overly dedicated
- Getting angry at you
- Accusing you
- Becoming helpless and confused
- Blaming others
- *Trying* instead of *Doing*
- Playing ignorant
- Being silent or acting hurt
- Crying, fainting, vomiting, bleeding
- Being very agreeable and cooperative
- Acting childlike and innocent
- Flattery or attention
- *Promising* instead of *delivering*
- Withdrawing
- Forgetting or being late
- Being too busy or having no time

What to remember when working with manipulations:
Stay calm when blocking a manipulation. Don't reject the manipulator. Manipulation occurs only when it works. Not all manipulation is conscious. You can't prevent, avoid, or stop another's manipulation. Use your feelings as an antenna to judge whether or not you are being manipulated. If you feel you are, you are. When one manipulation does not work, there will be a backup strategy. Do not quit in your efforts. The manipulator is talented. Manipulations will continue until healthier methods are developed. Some manipulations represent serious emotional problems. When in doubt that you are being manipulated, buy time. You have permission to put off decisions. Manipulation gets worse before it gets better. If things deteriorate, it is not a sign that you have failed, rather that you have succeeded. The manipulator is bringing out bigger guns. Do not let manipulations wear you down. You, as a change agent, need much strength. People use a great deal of force and strength in maintaining resistance.

What people have to recognize before they'll change:

1. That their thinking and behavior is self-defeating.
2. This is caused from something and didn't just magically appear.
3. Accept responsibility for the behavior and recognize that they started it and are carrying it along.
4. Even if their parents gave them these beliefs, they are now choosing to carry them themselves and keep affecting themselves by them.
5. They can do something about it.
6. Understand that they have to work at change. Must forcefully and repetitively dispute and challenge beliefs and practice substituting.
7. They can think and act their way out of it when they want to.

 Look back over any notes you've made in the margins in this chapter. Condense them into two action points; two changes you will make as a result of reading this section.

Actions to take:

1._____

2._____

Plant Your Feet Firmly in Mid-Air

Chapter Fifteen
Overcoming Resistance

Ancient philosophers have argued that even people who choose to change, resist their own efforts and resist their mentor's efforts as well.

There are three choices in overcoming resistance in others—guess which is the most natural?

1. Changing the other person
2. Changing the situation
3. Changing yourself

ANSWERS:

1 =This is the most natural but least effective. It builds resistance.

2 =This is a 50-50 proposition. It could go either way. Unless behavior is changed, one is always victim to creating situations in order to change things.

3 =This is the most difficult, yet most effective strategy.

**To overcome resistance,
do the opposite of what's expected.**

Six Tips for Dealing with Resistant People

Chances are, you are angry with the person you view as resistance to you. Correct? When you get angry at someone, *look to yourself first*. You are causing the anger because of something you are not taking care of, such as standing up for yourself ... or that other person is reminding you of a part of yourself that you would rather not accept as being there.

Similarly, if someone is angry with you, he is upset with himself. So just as your anger has little to do with the other person, his anger toward you has little to do with you.

1. Acknowledge the other person's hurt. Listen to what he or she is saying never ignore or laugh off genuine anger.

2. Show empathy. Communicate your concern by answering angry outbursts with something like "This is an upsetting matter—I can see why you're mad."

3. Be patient. Don't hurry up or shut up the angry person, even if it's painful to listen. Often merely expressing anger is therapeutic; let the person get it off his chest.

4. Stay cool. Remind yourself that highly agitated people say things they don't really mean. If something really damaging is said, respond to it only after the crisis is past.

If you embarrass someone, you will never again be able to work with that person

5. Talk about solutions. Once the most violent anger has subsided—and it should if you remain calm and compassionate—steer the conversation toward solving the underlying problem. If the other person is still too upset to look at things rationally, make sure she does nothing at all. Don't let angry people act on impulse.

6. Agree on a plan of action. When the other person has a grip on himself, settle on a specific solution to the problem, and agree on a timetable for implementation.

How to Say No

The ability to set limits and to place boundaries around oneself are absolutely necessary skills for tomorrow.

Communicate boundaries with an easy five-step process:

1. Acknowledge Understanding
"I understand you want me to take over the new account. That would involve overseeing production and working closely with the client."

2. Leave some room for discussion:
"I'd like to pass on this right now, although I appreciate the opportunity."

3. Offer explanations: lack of time, experience, resources, etc. Some of these may be negotiable.

4. Offer alternatives: "I might be able to take over the account in two or three months," or "I think Kirsten would be the ideal person to handle this."

5. Reaffirm your commitment to the company and its objectives: "I know the Sun account is very important to the company, and I'd like it to get the attention it deserves."

To overcome resistance, do the opposite of what's expected.

#1 Change Yourself

How often have you heard these sentences?
She's got an attitude problem.
Will you please listen and do as I say?
How do you motivate people anyway?
How do I get through to him?
You'd better straighten out!

You think life will get better as soon if only she changes, besides it's for *her* good, and you're only trying to help. Our life task is to get other people to change to the way we think they should be, because we know, right?

If you disagree more than 10 minutes, you're arguing about a deeper issue. If you are upset with something for more than 24 hours, you must deal with it directly and clear it up.

1. Stop getting mad at resistance.
Somebody isn't doing what you want. You feel frustrated, anxious, irritated, blocked, resentful. How successful you are depends on your attitude toward resistance. You want something from somebody else, and get frustrated when you don't get it. What happens you punish the other person exactly what the other person doesn't want, in a effort to get what you want. .

A woman heavily-laden with packages blocked my path during the boarding process at the Dallas airport a month or so ago. She stopped to unload just in front of me, blocking my path. Slowly she reached up to check the overhead bin. Even more slowly she took the shoulder strap of her bag off her shoulder and surveyed the scene for what seemed to be an eternity of time. She was relaxed, comfortable, even cheerful. I was impatient, frustrated, annoyed with her slowness, and by then probably hypertensive. Finally, she finished, and I brushed by her. it took much of the flight to settle down. On the way off the plane, guess who was right in front of me? The same thing happened in reverse, as she slowly and painstakingly removed her bags from the overhead bin and placed them on her shoulders. I pushed past eventually and rushed to the bathroom, indignant that in fact, these people had been allowed to survive during the last mass extinction on our planet. Then, as I was leaving the washroom, I stopped dead in my tracks. The package woman was standing in the exit to the washroom. Finally, I got it. I recognized that the problem didn't lay with her at all, in fact, *she* was doing beautifully. The problem lay with *me*, with my attitude, and my impatience with those who didn't flow neatly into my world .It was then that I recalled Kepler's Fourth Law: *The world does not revolve around you, you know.*

Chances are we hate or resent the person or situation that's resisting us. We get mad at it because it's the only way we can feel any power over it. Mad makes worse.

Resistance is healthy. If a medium in which you wish to create offers no resistance, there can be no durable impression. Put your finger in a bowl of water, then in ball of clay only one gives you permanent change

Let people resist you. If your two-year-old says no, you may take it as a declaration of war, rather than a healthy growing independence.

*Your attitude toward resistance
will determine how successful you are in dealing with it.*

If getting angry gives you power, it means you don't believe you have enough natural power.Also, when children are resisting you, they're getting stronger, and that is positive.

2. Make yourself appear trustworthy. Most managers assume that others understand their commitments, their basic honesty and that they mean well. In the absence of information, or communication about what is happening, most people fear the worst. It's a natural adaptive response to change. When there is low information, the situation is seen as more dangerous, and employees sense the worst. They will communicate this through the whole herd who then will be on alert. Unless you create conditions so that others know that you are trustworthy, expect the worst.

Deliberately create and keep small commitments. Decide on the few values that are important to your organization, stick to them, and make your decisions around them.

3. Learn the other person's (or department's, or company's) belief system. Supposing you are a salesperson for Lexus, you will never be able to convince your prospect despite the evidence that your product is superior. A series of questions will help expose one or more beliefs that, unless changed, will prevent sales. Belief might be that Japanese cars are inferior. If that's the belief, get beneath it to uncover basis for the belief, and only then can you provide evidence that Japanese cars are superior. People resist breaking their beliefs. Their behaviors must be in line with it.

That's why programs such as TQM, can't work unless the system beliefs are in line. Supposing a company's beliefs are that employees are lazy, and unless forced to do certain work will goof off. This will be reflected in enforcing time rules, punching clocks, supervising bathroom visits, limiting bathroom visits, taking out water coolers and coffee stations, refusing to allow interpersonal time in the halls, How easy will it be for that company to learn to delegate and share power.

3.Get into their belief systems. To shift their belief systems, get into their shoes and see the world the way they see it. Validate that it makes sense to see it that way. Until someone else validates it, they cannot let it go, because it doesn't make sense. Whenever something doesn't make sense have to stay with it until it does. This is the basis of post-trauma, everyday recollections, and the wake-up-at-3 AM experiences–we are trying to make sense or provide coherent explanation for something that has happened outside our range of understanding.

4. Show them what they need to do to learn new behaviors.
People resist stuff because they don't know how.

> *If you want to convert someone to your view, go over to where he is standing, take him by the hand mentally and guide him. Don't stand across the room and yell at him, don't call him a dummy, don't order him to come over where you are. You start where he is, and move from that position.*
> Thomas Aquinas

5. Allow others to become involved in the idea so it becomes theirs. Involvement reduces resistance. Surveys do not decrease resistance and are not an adequate form of involvement. Why? Because so much resistance has been built up to surveys because the history of lack of response. Why bother they're not going to do anything about them anyway?

6. Satisfy unmet interests.
Put yourself in the other's shoes ... would you change if you didn't have to? What interests make him want to say no? To the degree that you give others what they need they will give you what you need. People never get enough of what they don't need. What they want never satisfies them.

People want	They need
Sympathy	Empathy
Riches	Fulfillment
Fame	Recognition
Power	Support and cooperation
Dominate	Influence and guide
Prestige	Respect
Freedom	Discipline

7. Be patient
Change doesn't happen when we want it. it happens for it's own reason Nature changes only when it's forced to. A lobster sheds its shell, a rose bursts, a cocoon opens only when it's time.

When it's time, pour the wine.
Oscar Wilde

If you're living with an alcoholic, and you're making it easy for him, he'll never change. Your nagging makes it easier for him to drink because he's got an excuse–who wouldn't drink? People who resist because of denial need to a. Have insight and b. Wake up in the gutter, which means not be spared the consequences of their own actions.

Change happens only after crises. A 50-year-old woman refuses to quit her 3-pack-a-day habit until she is diagnosed with lung cancer and has one lung removed. A 66-year-old-man in Corbin, Kentucky had to shut down his restaurant, but then hit the road offering herbs, spices and methods for best fried chicken in the south.

We often assume resistance when we haven't yet asked clearly for what we need. You may be assuming resistance when there is none.

Can you fill in the following?
I wish that my husband would ...
I wish my boss would ....
I wish my secretary would
I wish my neighbor would ...
I wish the city would ....

Ask For What you Need.
"When I speak to you, please don't yawn, watch TV, read the paper, stare at the clock because I feel unimportant and unlistened to. Look directly at me, nod occasionally, and when I am finished, paraphrase what I've said."

How many times during the day do you hear:

You'll have to ... you need to ... You'll have to get in the other line You'll have to sign the forms by Monday. . . You'll have to call back Tuesday . . . You'll have to ask George . . . You'll have to get permission. . . . You need to ask.

Communicating Change to Increase Cooperation

1. Start verbally, in small groups or one to one, then in writing. Start with natural leader of work group, people to whom others look for direction and advice. Groups can be better because everyone hears it at the same time.

2. Get input and then try to sell them what they wrote, keep control of decision making.

Resistance is an emotional process taking part in the other person. It's not a reflection of you. It's a predictable, natural emotional reaction.

> *Disarm by surprise: do the opposite of what is expected.*
> *Listen, acknowledge, and agree when you can.*
> *Whatever you want from him, you give first.*

 # How to Overcome Resistance

1. **Cognitive behavioral:** Challenge assumptions.

2. **Referenting:** List advantages of changing and not changing.

3. **Challenge people directly to change:** Use paradoxical questions like "Suppose you pick the wrong thing to do and work hard at it with little results. Why would that be a really good thing to do?" "I wonder what good things can result from working hard at something that fails?"

1. Trying and failing is better than not trying at all

2. Striving to change can lead to important information about the self that can be used later on or can instigate new change.

3. Action can feel good by itself, certainly better than no action. Even if it doesn't produce good results.

4. Can increase your frustration tolerance by accepting delayed results.

5. Principle of flow—when you're moving just beyond yourself.

Exercises

Role Reversal
Get the resistant persons to explain to others why they should change. For example, if one department resists a new idea, have them explain reasons for it. Then get them to try to sell the idea to another department. The process of teaching someone else to do something causes learning. If there are two persons in conflict, have them take each others' roles.

Distraction
Get them involved in an absorbing task like writing reports, member of force, volunteering to help others to change.

Specific Techniques

Overcome Resistance
Resisters have low frustration tolerance. They feel entitled, and want immediate gratification.Resisters promise to do things but then the results are meager, irregular, or not at all. Get them to pair up with a co-worker who isn't resistant. Marketing and engineering make good pairs.

Look back over any notes you've made in the margins in this chapter. Condense them into two action points; two changes you will make as a result of reading this section.

Actions to take:

1._____

2._____

Afterword

Nobody's an expert on change. We cannot make sense of change. It is inherently chaotic. But it will pass. Weather patterns change; trouble comes to pass, it doesn't come to stay. When you're flying along in a little airplane in life, and go through a thunderstorm, almost always the updrafts will get you out on the other side at a higher altitude. Just keep your wings level, slow down to reduce stress on the airframe, relax, and watch your instruments. The way out is the way through. Just remember not to flail around, give up, blame mother nature, or take it personally.

Follow the wisdom of my first flight instructor, John Alves, who said, "takeoffs are optional, but landings are mandatory." Once you've entered the storm, you can't go back–you cannot undo what you've already done. The world has permanently changed. Keep flying, and trust your instruments. At the risk of sounding trite:

It is better now than it was.
You will make it.
Just keep moving.

References

Ackerman, L.S. (1986). Development, Transition, or
    Transformation: The Question of Change in Organizations.
    OD Practitioner, 18, 4, 1-5.
Bardwick, J. (1995). *Danger in the Comfort Zone.* New York:
    AMACOM.
Barker, J. (1992). *Future Edge.* New York: William Morrow &
    Co, Inc.
Bastien, D.T. (1987). Common Patterns of Behavior and
    Communications in Corporate Mergers and Acquisitions.
    Human Resource Management, Spring.
Berger, L. & Sikora, M. (1994). *The Change Management
    Handbook.* New York: Irwin Professional Publishing.
Block, P. (1993). *Stewardship.* San Francisco: Berrett-Koehler.
Bridges, W. (1980). *Transitions.* Reading, Mass: Addison-Wesley.
Bridges, W. (1994). *Job Shift.* Reading, MA: Addison-Wesley.
Burrus, D. (1993). *TechnoTrends.* New York: HarperBusiness.
Chandler, R. (1992). *Racing Towards 2001.* San Francisco:
    HarperSan Francisco.
Collins, J. & Porras, J. (1994). *Built To Last.* New York:
    HarperCollins.
Conger, J., Kanungo, R. et al. (1988). *Charismatic Leadership.*
    San Francisco: Jossey-Bass.
Csikszentmihalyi, M. (1990). *Flow.* New York: HarperPerennial.

Davidson, J. (1991). *Breathing Space*. New York: Mastermedia.

Davidow, W. H., & Malone, M.S. (1992). *The Virtual Corporation*. New York: HarperBusiness.

Davis, S. & Davidson, B. (1991). *2020 Vision*. New York: Simon & Schuster.

Davis, S. M. (1987). *Future Perfect: A Startling Vision of the Future We Should Be Managing Now*. Reading, MA: Addison-Wesley.

Dawson, R. (1995). *Secrets of Power Negotiating*. Hawthorne: Career Press.

DeMills, D.Q. & Friesen, G.B. (1996). *Broken Promises: An unconventional view of what went wrong at IBM*. Boston, MA: Harvard Business School Press.

Deming, W. E. (1986). *Out of the Crisis*. Cambridge, MA: MIT Center Advanced Engineering.

Drucker, P. (1980). *Managing in Turbulent Times*. New York: HarperRow.

DuBrin, A.J. (1996). *Reengineering Survival Guide*. Cincinatti, Ohio: Thomson Executive Press.

Ellis, A. (1985). *Overcoming Resistance*. New York: Springer Publishing.

Farkas, C. M. & DeBacker, P. (1996). *The World's Leading CEO's share their Strategies for Success*. New York: Henry Holt.

Ferguson, M. (1980). *The Aquarian Conspiracy*. Los Angeles: J.P. Tarcher.

Gersick, C. J. (1991). Revolutionary Change Theories: A Multilevel Exploration of the Punctuated Equilibrium Paradigm, *Academy of Management Review*, 16, 1, pp.10-36.

Grove, A. (1996). *Managing the S-Curve*. New York: Doubleday.

Hawken, P. (1993). *The Ecology of Commerce*. New York: HarperBusiness.

Hurst, D.K. (1995). *Crisis & Renewal: Meeting the Challenge of Organizational Change*. Boston, Mass: Harvard Business School Press.

Hamel, G. & Prahalad, C.K. *(1994)*. *Competing for the Future*. Boston, MA: Harvard Business School Press.

Hammer, M. & Champy, J. (1993). *Reengineering the Corporation*. New York: HarperCollins.

Harvey, J. (1988). *The Abilene Paradox*. New York, Lexington.

Hawken, P. (1993). *The Ecology of Commerce*. New York: HarperBusiness.

Hurst, D.K. (1996). *Crisis & Renewal: Meeting the Challenge of Organizational Change*. Boston, MA: Harvard Business School Press.

Johansell, R. & Swigart, R. (1994). *Upsizing the Individual in the Downsized Organization*. Reading, MA: Addison-Wesley.

Kanfer, F. & Goldstein, A. (1986). *Helping People Change*. New York: Pergamon Press, Inc.

Kaplan, R.S. & Norton, D.P. (1996). *The Balanced Scorecard is more than just a New Measurement System*.Boston, Mass: Harvard Business School Press.

Katzenbach, J.R. (1996). *Real Change Leaders*. New York: Times Business.

Katzenbach, J.R. & Smith, D.K. (1990). *The Wisdom of Teams: Creating the high-performance organization*. New York: Times Business.

Kestin, H. (1992). *21st Century Management*. New York: Atlantic Monthly Press.

Kosko, B. (1993). *Fuzzy Thinking*. New York: Hyperion.

Kriegel, R. (1995). *Facilitation of Change*. In L.R. Pondy et al. (Eds.) *Organizational Symbolism*, Greenwich, CT: JAI Press.

Lakoff, G. & Johnson, M. (1980). *Metaphors We Live By*, Chicago: The University of Chicago Press.

Lapp, J. (1994). *Dancing with Tigers*. New York: Demeter Books.

Larkin, T.J. & Larkin, S. (1994). *Communicating Change: Winning Employee Support for new Business Goals*. New York: McGraw Hill.

Larkin, T.J. & Larkin, S. (1996). Reaching and Changing Frontline employees. *Harvard Business Review*, May-June, pp. 95-109.

LeBoeuf, M. (1994). *Fast Forward: How to Win a Lot More Business in a Lot Less Time*. New York: Berkley Books.

LeBoeuf, M. (1989). *How to Win Customers and Keep Them for Life*.New York: Berkley Books.

MacCormac, E.R. (1976). *Metaphor and Myth in Science and*

Religion, Durham, N.C.: Duke University Press.

McLelland, D.C. (1978). Managing Motivation to Expand Human Freedom. *American Psychologist, 33*, 201-210.

McLuhan, M. & Fiore, Q. (1966). *The Medium is the Message.* New York: Bantam.

Moore, P. (1994). Turning the Tide at Whirpool. *Communication World,* March.

Morgan, G. (1986). *Images of Organization.* Beverly Hills, CA: Sage Publications, Inc.

Morrison, I. (1996). *The Second Curve.* New York: Ballantine.

Morrison, F. & Schmid, G. (1994). *Future Tense: Preparing for the Business Realities in the Next Ten Years.* New York: Morrow.

Nanus, B. (1992). *Visionary Leadership.* San Francisco: Jossey-Bass.

Nilson, C. (1995). *Games That Drive Change.* New York: McGraw-Hill.

Nocera, J. (1994). *A Piece of the Action: How the Middle Class joined the Money Class.* New York: Simon & Schuster, 1994.

O'Hara-Devereaux, M., & Johansen, R. (1994). *Globalwork: Bridging Distance, Culture, and Time.* San Francisco: Jossey-Bass.

Osborne, D. and Gaebler, T. (1993). *Reinventing Government.* New York: Penguin Books.

O'Toole, J. (1985). *Vanguard Management: Redesigning the Corporate Future.* Garden City, NJ: Doubleday.

Overholt, W. (1993). *The Rise of China: How Economic Reform Is Creating a New Superpower.* New York: Norton.

Peters, T. (1987). *Thriving on Chaos.* New York: Knopf.

Peters, T. and Waterman, R. (1982). *In Search of Excellence.* San Francisco: Harper and Row.

Pfeffer, J. (1966) Competitive Advantage through People: Unleashing the power of the work force. In P.L. Berger and T. Luckmann, (Eds.) *The Social Construction of Reality,* Garden City, NY: Doubleday.

Rachlis, M. and Kushner, C. (1994). *Strong Medicine.* Toronto: HarperCollins.

Reichheld, F.F. & Teal, T. (1996). *The Loyalty Effect: The hidden force behind growth, profits, and lasting value.* Boston, MA: Harvard Business School Press.

Marshak, R.J. & Katz, J.H. (1992). The Symbolic Side of OD. *OD Practitioner, 24,* 2, pp.1-5.

Richter, T. (1996). *How to Have a Life and Keep your Car Clean, Too.* Monterey, CA: Bayview Press

Rothschild, M. (1992). *Bionomics: Economy as Ecosystem.* New York: Henry Holt.

St. James, E. (1996). *Living the Simple Life: A Guide to Scaling Down and Enjoying More.* New York: Hyperion.

Sapenian, A. (1994). *Regional Advantage: Culture and Competition in Silicon Valley and Route 128.* Cambridge, Mass: Harvard University Press.

Schacter, S.& Singer, J.E. (1962). Cognitive, social, and physiological determinants of emotional state. *Psychological Review, 69,* 379-399.

Schein, E.H. (1985). *Organizational Culture and Leadership,* San Francisco: Jossey Bass Publishers.

Seligman, M. (1990). *Learned Optimism.* New York: Pocket Books.

Shepp, B. & Shepp, D. (1995) *The Telecommuter's Handbook.* New York: McGraw-Hill.

Siegelman, E.Y. (1990). *Metaphor and Meaning in Psychotherapy,* New York: The Guilford Press.

Senge, P. (1990). *The Fifth Discipline.* New York: Currency-Doubleday.

Senge, P., Kleiner, A., Roberts, C., Ross, R. and Smith, B. (1994). *The Fifth Discipline Fieldbook.* New York: Currency-Doubleday.

Sherman, V. (1993). *Creating the New American Hospital.* San Francisco: Jossey-Bass.

Simon, H. (1996). *Hidden Champions: Lessons from 500 of the world's best unknown companies.* Boston, MA: Harvard Business School Press.

Slywotzky, A.J. (1996). *Value Migration: How to think several moves ahead of the competition.* Boston, MA: Harvard Business School Press.

Smith, D. (1996). *Taking Charge of Change.* New York: Addison Wesley.

Strebel, P. (1996). Why do employees resist change? *Harvard Business Review*, May-June, pp. 86-94.

Strebel, P. (1997). *New Personal Compacts: The Missing Link to Change Management*. Boston, MA: Harvard Business School Press.

Tannen, D. (1990).*You Just Don't Understand*. New York: Ballantine.

Taylor, D. & Archer, J.S. (1994). *Up Against the Wal-Marts*. New York: AMACOM.

Tomasko, R. (1993). *Rethinking the Corporation*. New York: AMACOM.

Treacy, M. & Wierseman, F. (1995). *The Discipline of Market Leaders*. New York: Addison Wesley.

Tsoukas, H. (1991). The Missing Link: A Transformational View of Metaphors in Organizational Science, *Academy of Management Review*, 16, 3, pp. 566-585.

Walton, M. (1990). *Deming Management at Work*. New York: Perigree Books.

Weiss, A. (1995). *Our Emperors Have No Clothes*. Franklin Lakes: Career Press.

Wilson, L. (1987). *Changing the Game: The New Way to Sell*. New York: Simon & Schuster.

Wurman, R. (1989). *Information Anxiety*. New York: Ballantine.

Index

About the Author

A native Canadian from Montreal, Quebec, **Dr. Janet Lapp** has been a registered nurse and nurse manager, with several years experience in direct health care and healthcare management. She graduated magna cum laude in clinical psychology, and completed a Ph.D. with Honours from McGill University in Montreal. Awarded a post-doctoral fellowship, she went on to a successful career as a clinician and university professor.

Now, **Dr. Janet Lapp** is one of North America's most celebrated professional speakers. She is the creator and host of the highly-rated CBS series "Keep Well," and has created or appeared in several documentaries and training films. As President of CLD International, a worldwide communications and leadership development firm, she consults with leaders worldwide, helping them overcome others' resistance to change. She is the publisher of *The Change Letter*, a guide to helping business adjust to the future.

Her in-house training programs have resulted from evidence that the leading cause of wasted productivity and employee illness, is workplace stress caused by poor conflict resolution and communication skills.

Termed 'the solution to our current energy crisis,' **Dr. Janet's** energy-charged, exhilarating programs give useable ideas to put to work right away in helping people and business groups adjust to the current and future workplace.

Educational Materials by Dr. Janet Lapp

Plant Your Feet Firmly in Mid-Air Series

Plant Your Feet Firmly in Mid-Air, Book, 256 pages	22.95
Plant Your Feet Firmly in Mid-Air, 6-cassette program, workbook	59.95
Plant Your Feet Firmly in Mid-Air Video Program	
Part I Staying Focused During Change	39.95
Part II Future Trends	39.95
Part III Managing Others Reactions to Change	39.95
Complete Video Set (Parts I-III)	**99.95**

Complete Package

Hardcover Book, 6-cassette program and complete video set

$175.00

Dancing with Tigers Series

Dancing with Tigers, Book, 123 pages	10.95
Dancing with Tigers, 6-cassette program, workbook	59.95

The Change Letter: *A Quarterly Guide to Adjusting to the Future*

	$75.00/year
For Dr. Lapp's program attendees:	$35.00/year

Order from your local bookstore, book distributor or directly from:

Lapp & Associates
Post Office Box 2583, Del Mar, California 92014
Orders: (800) 435-2927• (619) 792-8206• Fax (619) 792-8236

Name:_____

Company:_____

Address:_____

City/Zip/State:_____

Phone: (   ) _____ Fax: (   ) _____

Payment: Check enclosed ❏ or VISA ❏   MC ❏   Amexco ❏

Card No.:_____ Exp. Date: _____

Signature: _____

Print Name: (as it appears on card)_____

Calif residents, please add
applicable sales tax

PACKING/SHIPPING CHARGES	
Up to $30.00	$4.50
$30.01–$60.00	$5.50
Over $60.00	$6.50

Summary Notes

_____

_____

_____

_____

_____

_____

_____

_____

_____

_____

_____

_____

_____

_____

_____

_____

_____

_____

_____

_____

_____

_____

_____

_____

_____

_____